THE AMAZING BASKETBALL BOOK:

THE FIRST 100 YEARS

by Bob Hill
and Randall Baron

Published by
Full Court Press
a division of
Devyn Press, Inc.
Louisville, Kentucky

Cover photo credits:
Photo by Pam Spaulding
Separations by Rick Covalciuc
Typesetting by Betty Mattison
Lighting by Gary Chapman
Design by Steve Sebree
Shot by Cindy Stucky
Peach Basket by Louisville Farmers' Market
Basketball by Jeffersonville (Ind.) High School
  Ralph Scales, Athletic Director
  Mark Bixler, Coach

Printed in the United States of America.

Devyn Press, Inc.
151 Thierman Lane
Louisville, KY 40207

ISBN 0-910791-42-2

Table of Contents

Dedication

To Janet, who has endured a lot more than a book about basketball.
Bob Hill

To Dorsey, Bruce, Ralph and Leeland,
"I get by with a little help from my friends."
John Lennon and Paul McCartney
Randall Baron

Acknowledgments

Special thanks go to the Naismith Memorial Basketball Hall of Fame, especially Joe O'Brien, executive director, June Steitz, and Wayne Patterson, for their time, advice, photos, and use of their library; Pam Spaulding, who provided the cover photos, as well as copies of most inside photos; Pat Howington, for his invaluable editing help; and Betty Mattison of Devyn Graphics for her typesetting and patience.

We are also indebted to the following people for their help in producing this book:

Lisa Barker	Mike Covington	Mimi Maier
Ralph Bergmann	Mike Freeman	Mike Mangeot
Cherie Cova	Tony Lipka	Bonnie Baron Pollack
Rick Covalciuc	Mary Anne Maier	Steve Sebree

Photo Credits

Page 51 is by Ford Reid.
Page 52 (left) National Federation of State High School Associations
Page 52 (right) Iowa Girls' Athletic Association
Page 72, 88 (right), 131, 138 (right), 154 University of Kentucky Sports Information Dept.
Page 79 Rawlings Sporting Goods Co.
Page 80 (right), 88, 101, 105, 166, 199 are reprinted with the permission of *The Courier Journal*.
Page 144 is by Bob Hill.
All other photographs are courtesy of the Naismith Memorial Basketball Hall of Fame.

Introduction

OK, this isn't really the 100th anniversary of the invention of basketball.

Doc Naismith didn't nail up his first peach basket until December, 1891, so the official centennial celebration is still a few double dribbles down the calendar.

So what! Basketball is such a great game we couldn't wait that long.

We wanted to tell you how basketball got started, why the goal is ten feet off the floor, and that the real hero was a janitor named "Pop" Stebbins who hunted up some peach baskets when Naismith actually had square wooden boxes in mind.

That's how close basketball came to being "boxball."

We bet you didn't know that Naismith was a Canadian of Scottish descent, a high school dropout, and that he authored the 13 original rules of basketball in about an hour, or less time than it takes Dick Vitale to finish a sentence.

We're positive you didn't know that although Naismith invented basketball, he lived another 48 years and only played it twice.

There's a lot of other amazing stuff in this book, too!

Do you know which of The Doc's original 13 rules are still in effect?

Do you know why basketball players were called "cagers?"

Can you name America's all-time high school scoring stars?

Do you know the one-eyed University of Arkansas hotshot who set an all-time NCAA free throw shooting record?

Do you realize the three-point goal is actually 96 years old?

Can you name the first woman, and the first black, to be drafted by the National Basketball Association?

Do you know why you're reading this instead of doing something important?

It's because you care about basketball, or you know someone who does. You want to know why it took the pioneers of the game almost 15 years to learn life would proceed much more smoothly if someone would cut a hole in the bottom of the basket so the ball could fall through.

That's the purpose of "The Amazing Basketball Book." It's 208 pages of classic photographs, wonderful anecdotes, funny stories and lovingly irreverent — but always accurate — basketball history.

It covers the court from James Naismith to Bobby Knight.

So don't just sit there, basketball fans, get out there and read!

THANKS, DOC!

Foreword

As he walked through the empty gymnasium of the International YMCA Training School in Springfield, Massachusetts, 30-year-old James Naismith had a problem to solve. He had to invent a new game to keep his students happy. He had to invent what would become basketball.

It's impossible now to imagine life without basketball. There wasn't a Magic Johnson, Larry Bird or David Robinson. There wasn't an Adolph Rupp, Dean Smith or Pat Riley. There were no state high school or college basketball tournaments. There was only an empty school gymnasium, and winter.

Naismith changed that forever. He gave us whatever emotions we feel as a Michael Jordan climbs toward the basket, or a coach like Jim Valvano runs madly around a basketball floor in all directions celebrating an NCAA basketball championship.

He gave us the hurt we feel as the local team loses the state high school championship by one point.

He created most of this in just one day in December, 1891, and the magic evolved from there. He picked up a round ball, asked a janitor to find something in which to toss it, and jotted down some rules based on games he'd played as a child. He was very proud of his game, but really had no idea what he had done. As he would later write, he was just trying to find a solution to a problem.

His solution has since sent millions of people around the world into playing arenas that vary from church basements to 75,000-seat stadiums. It has sent North Dakota farm boys outside in below-zero weather to shoot jump shots at tractor-wheel hoops, and made millionaires out of children of the ghetto.

His game survived so many turns and narrow escapes we're lucky it got here at all. As you will see, much the same thing can be said about its inventor.

Chapter 1
SALOONS AND
SEMINARY SCHOOL
The amazing early life of
James Naismith

James A. Naismith, The Father of Basketball, was born November 6, 1861, in a farmhouse near Almonte, Ontario, about 60 miles north of New York State.

It seems fitting that The Doc was born at what is now the beginning of basketball season, and in a rural setting that is so synonomous with the early roots of the game.

The only more satisfying history would have been to have Naismith born in a manger somewhere in Kentucky or Indiana.

The Doc didn't have an easy early life. In 1869, his father, John, a Scottish farmer and laborer, moved his family from Ontario to the neighboring province of Quebec, where he had invested in a sawmill. The family included his wife, Margaret, and his three children, Annie, James and Robert.

In the summer of 1870 a fire destroyed the sawmill, claiming all the family's money. That fall typhoid fever swept through many of the Canadian lumber camps, and the Naismith family was in its terrible path.

The fever hit John Naismith first. He lived only a few days before dying on October 19, 1870. Margaret Naismith died three weeks later. The date was November 6, James' ninth birthday.

The three Naismith children were taken back to a farm near Almonte to live, eventually moving in with a bachelor uncle, a strong discipliarian named Peter Young.

It was a difficult, relentless pioneer life, with all children expected to do chores, chop trees for firewood and work in the fields behind the big draft horses.

During the quiet time at night Naismith also played the violin — his first true contact with string music.

The Doc, as his father before him, grew up tough, resourceful, and exceptionally strong. But he was an indifferent student, and after walking the three miles to Almonte for one year to attend high school, he dropped out in the fall of his second year. He was 15, and said he saw no need in learning more than he already knew.

That was basketball's first close call! If The Doc had held to that belief, you have to wonder what the rest of us would now be doing for entertainment from December through March.

For several years after he dropped out of school Naismith worked in the Canadian logging camps during the winter and on the family farm during

Opposite page: This picture of Dr. James Naismith was taken in 1936 after he returned from the Olympics in Berlin. He went into the school that day and talked to the children, telling them that playing Duck on a Rock on the stone (a large granite boulder) across the corner from the Almonte school had given him the idea of the upward toss in basketball.

the summer. He was headstrong and independent, but he also knew that his orphaned brother and sister needed his financial support.

But as a lumberjack, he naturally adopted a lifestyle that included coarse language and the imbibing of demon rum in Almonte's thriving saloon. At that point the odds that this brawny, whiskey-tipping Canadian lumberjack would ever get around to inventing America's Game seemed very remote indeed.

Yet beneath The Doc's heavy boots, plaid shirts and rough-talking lumberjack demeanor beat a heart as pure as a three-on-one fast break.

At age 20 he finally came to his senses, put down the whiskey glass, picked up his school books and went back to Almonte High School for his second year of study.

It was not a totally popular decision at home because Naismith's Uncle Peter still needed him for the farm work, but Naismith said he thought he could handle both.

Thank you, Doc. Thank you. Thank you. Thank you.

With the help of a marvelous principal, Peter McGregor, Naismith pushed through high school in two years. He also passed his Latin and Greek exams, which qualified him to attend Canadian universities.

His story would be an inspiration for a high school drop-out of any era, but Naismith's was only beginning; he wanted to go on to college. The bad news was that Uncle Peter still needed him at home.

A compromise was reached. The Doc could go to college if, as Uncle Peter wanted, he became a Presbyterian minister, and if Naismith agreed to work summers on the farm.

So in the fall of 1883 The Doc enrolled in McGill University in Montreal, perhaps the finest university in Canada. He was 22 years old, and the invention of basketball was only eight years away.

McGill was a university that cultivated religion, and Naismith was a young man with seminary school on his mind. But he was too much a natural athlete to be tucked away in some corner of the school library.

At the urging of some friends he discovered the gymnasium, and with a little practice learned that his farmboy strength could easily be turned into gymnastic exercises, and then, inevitably, rugby football.

Naismith took to rugby like Akeem Olajuwon to a slam jam. He soon became a minor legend on the McGill team, while also developing some sense of the joy of intercollegiate competition.

In 1887 he graduated in the top ten in his class with a Bachelor of Arts in philosophy and Hebrew. He was 25 years old, and the invention of basketball was only four years away.

After graduating from McGill, Naismith moved into its nearby Presbyterian

10

The Doc — 1892

College, where he became a seminary student. He also continued to be heavily involved in athletics, including a brief stint with a professional lacrosse team.

This, of course, was long before the era of Oral Roberts University and the Fighting Irish of Notre Dame. Contact sports and calm religious pursuit were not supposed to mix. Naismith's athletic activities, especially when pursued by such a muscular seminary student wielding a lacrosse stick, scared the devil out of his more docile colleagues.

But Naismith did not want to give up either athletics or religion. He wanted to find a place where he could blend the two. He strongly believed a spiritual emphasis was very possible in the unsavory world of physical education. Many of his classmates thought him loony.

Naismith, ever stubborn, left the Presbyterian College in 1890. He had enough credits to graduate as an honor student, but did not become an ordained minister. That wouldn't happen until 25 years later.

Naismith's departure was a very controversial move, especially with his Uncle Peter. However, The Doc didn't maintain his free agent status very long. He immediately signed with the Young Men's Christian Association, which was mixing athletics and Christian thought at a school in Springfield, Massachusetts, called the International Young Men's Christian Association Training School — good old IYMCATS.

The Doc — many years later.

And how do you think today's basketball cheerleaders would deal with that one?

"Gimmie an "I" . . .

"Gimmie an "N" . . .

"Gimmie a "T" . . .

It would take a Broadway choreographer 45 minutes to get the cheer finished.

But hang on, Hoop Fans, because The Doc was on a roll, and the invention of basketball was only about a year away.

FIVE MORE AMAZING FACTS ABOUT
THE DOC'S EARLY LIFE

★ The Doc's debut in rugby football was like something out of a Ronald Reagan movie. In the autumn of 1884, his second year at McGill, he was watching rugby practice when one of the regulars had his nose accidently rearranged. The Doc had never played rugby before, but on request from one of the team captains Naismith tossed off his coat and ran into the fray. The next Saturday he was in the starting lineup.

★ The Doc's daughter-in-law, Grace Naismith, claimed that he eventually acquired 11 degrees, both actual and honorary. These included degrees in Greek, Hebrew, music and philosophy.

★ The crest on Naismith's football jersey read "In Domino Confido" or "Trust in God," but after one particularly trying game Naismith had to ascend into the student minister's pulpit with two black eyes.

★ The Doc played in the center of the rugby football line at 160 pounds for eight years and never missed a game.

★ Life on the Canadian frontier could be incredibly harsh. On December 31, 1884, New Year's Eve, Naismith and his brother, Robbie, went to bed early in anticipation of the usual 5 a.m. wakeup call to go logging, even during the Christmas holidays. That night Robbie complained of a terrible stomach ache and his sister, Annie, tried the usual home remedy, a dose of salts. Robbie died an hour later of a ruptured appendix.

Chapter 2
"POP" STEBBINS
AND PEACH BASKETS
The amazing saga of what might have been boxball

Gymnasium in the School for Christian Workers, where the first basketball scrimmage took place December, 1891.

Let us briefly review the film clips of James Naismith's early life: he was orphaned at nine, dropped out of high school at 15 to become a whiskey-tipping lumberjack, went back to high school at 20, and didn't even discover organized, intercollegiate athletics until age 22.

Six years later he was employed at the Young Men's Christian Association in Springfield, Massachusetts, trying to mix rigorous exercise and religion.

Which led him, of course, to invent basketball.

So hold onto that thought for at least 24 seconds: basketball, the game we all know and love, the game that we now see as practically a public trust, a game played in 9,000-seat high school gymnasiums, 24,000-seat college facilities, and 50,000-seat professional arenas, began in the dinky basement of a Christian training school as a recreational activity for a bunch of would-be teachers.

Basketball didn't last long in that environment. Within 20 years some YMCAs had begun to ban the game, calling it a sport for unchristian rowdies.

But that, Christian soldiers, is where it began.

Gimmie a "Y" . . .

Gimmie an "M" . . .

Gimmie a "C" . . .

Gimmie an "A" . . .

Naismith didn't invent basketball in his first ten minutes on the job. He went to work in Springfield in September, 1890, with plenty of other things to do.

The school had been built in 1885 to house both the Armory Hill YMCA and the YMCA's training school, also known as the School for Christian Workers. The school had about 40 students and it was Naismith's job to keep them busy.

One of the students was Amos Alonzo Stagg, an early American athletic hero while at Yale University, who would go on to win more than 300 games as a football coach.

Stagg eventually coached football at the Springfield YMCA, playing such East Coast colleges as Harvard and Yale, which was standard practice at the time. In fact, his Springfield team almost whipped Yale in the first football game ever played indoors, an 1890 clash inside the original Madison Square Garden in New York.

Naismith played center on that Springfield football team, thus giving him two legs up on indoor sports history; he was present when the first football and the first basketball games were played indoors.

Naismith, a lifetime tinkerer, is also credited with inventing the first football helmet.

The Doc had already developed one cauliflower ear because of contact

The original basketball team that took part in the very first game, December 1891, at a YMCA training school in Springfield, Mass., is: front row, left to right: Finlay G. MacDonald, William H. Davis and Lyman W. Archibald. Second row: Frank Mahan and Doctor Naismith. Third row: John G. Thompson, Eugene S. Libby, Doctor Edwin P. Ruggles, William R. Chase and T. Duncan Patton, captain of this original basketball team.

sports, so he began wrapping a broad piece of tape around his head during football games.

This, while keeping his ears plastered against the side of his head, also gave him the general appearance of a survivor of Valley Forge.

So Naismith advanced the art a few turns, first by wrapping several layers of flannel around his head, and then fastening down the flannel with a piece of chamois, the latter tied under the chin like a bonnet.

This inventiveness was noticed by Dr. Luther Halsey Gulick, Jr., who was Naismith's boss at Springfield. Gulick's name doesn't surface much in basketball history, but it should; if James Naismith was the Father of Basketball then Gulick, in a slightly less literal sense, was certainly its Mother.

Gulick was a pioneer of building men through clean minds and strong, healthy bodies, a philosophy of life that was easily acceptable to Naismith.

Naismith had gone to Springfield just about the time intercollegiate sports such as football, track and baseball were beginning to become popular.

The problem — and this seems almost impossible to believe now — was that there was nothing interesting for the athletes to do between the end of football season and the beginning of baseball season.

There was only a black hole in the calendar where basketball should have been.

Gulick, only 25 himself, noticed this. He saw the students at his training school becoming bored with endless winter drills and gymnastic training, a boredom that made the classes very difficult to teach.

How, after all, can you keep a bunch of jocks happy if all they have to do for three months is toss Indian clubs at one another?

So in the fall of 1891 Gulick and The Doc had a conversation that went something like this:

"James, we badly need a new game that can be played indoors in the winter. How, after all, can we keep a bunch of jocks happy if all they have to do for three months is toss Indian clubs at one another?"

"I agree, sir," said Naismith. "A whole new game."

This building was occupied by the School for Christian Workers and the Armory Hill YMCA, when basketball was first played here in December, 1891. The door to the gallery of the gym is at the far left, showing the white steps on which the picture was taken of "The First Team."

"James, you are truly an inventive lad," said Gulick, pressing his advantage. "Anyone who can wrap bandages around his head and call it a football helmet must surely be capable of inventing a whole new game.

"But I think it should be done using elements of games we already know. And I don't want these guys killing each other or tearing up our gym. We are a Christian organization. Let's not forget that."

"OK, sir," said The Doc. "I'll give it a shot."

But Naismith didn't give it a shot right away. As eager, helpful and inventive as he was, he was already pretty busy with boxing, wrestling, swimming and canoeing.

His problems were compounded because Gulick had asked him to invent a new game especially for a class in the Secretarial Department of the Springfield training school.

He was to have the class for just 14 days. But these weren't kids who could be flim-flammed into any new game. They were grown men in their late 20s, and several of them threw a mean Indian club.

His first attempt at a new game was a combination of football, soccer and lacrosse; his roughneck charges nearly destroyed each other, and parts of the gymnasium, for his trouble.

For 13 days The Doc kept tinkering with different games, adding a goal here or a different rule there, but all he got was more and more discouraged.

He had worried and stewed, schemed and plotted, but nothing seemed to be working.

And then, on the 14th day — quite possibly December 21, 1891 — he invented basketball.

Talk about winning one at the buzzer!

Actually, Gulick had also asked the other members on the training school staff for their advice on a new game, but The Doc had cleared the best path to the goal right from the beginning.

He had agreed that the new game should combine the basic elements of existing games, but without the mayhem. That meant the athletes could not be allowed to run but must, instead, toss a ball to one another and then into . . . well, WHAT should they toss it into?

That was the question of the winter, if not the century. Naismith gave some thought to a lacrosse goal, but those were vertical, much too close to the gym floor and would probably encourage, not prevent, mayhem.

Then he remembered a childhood game "Duck on the Rock," during which the frisky Canadian lads would attempt to knock a softball-sized rock off a big boulder by lobbing smaller rocks at it from about 20 feet away.

Tossing rocks indoors didn't seem like a particularly safe way to pass the winter, but the concept of lobbing an arched shot toward a goal — the best

Duck on the Rock players always used arch — did appeal to Naismith.

So he combined that thought with another he'd had a few years earlier at McGill where he'd had the rugby team stay loose in the off-season by tossing balls into an empty box or basket set on the gym floor.

The McGill concept had its problems. Very few shots ever got into the box because the players would just surround it (inventing, of course, the first zone defense). But at Springfield The Doc suddenly solved most of his problems by looking no higher than the elevated running track around the inside of the training school gymnasium.

THAT was the answer: elevate the goal; put it well above the players' heads and let them lob the ball into it.

Wow! Whatta game!

OK, there were still a few details to be ironed out. What was The Doc going to do about double-dribbling, the three-second lane, the NCAA championships, recruiting scandals, summer camps, basketball shoe endorsements and Bobby Knight vs. Puerto Rico?

But his game was off and running, and the dramatic final scene would soon fall neatly into place.

For instance, The Doc was still having trouble deciding exactly what kind of ball to toss into his elevated goals. As he walked to his gymnasium office

From an early Spalding catalog.

19

THE FIRST GAME

A drawing of the first game. Note "Pop" Stebbins on the ladder.

U. S. postage stamp issued in 1961 to honor the 100th birthday anniversary of James Naismith.

Dr. Luther H. Gulick.

1940 students portray conditions of the first scrimmage of 1891.

on the morning of that fateful 14th day, he saw both a football and a soccer ball lying on the floor.

He grabbed, praise be to all things round, the soccer ball.

Can you imagine dribbling a football?

The Doc then headed for the gymnasium, intent on asking ''Pop'' Stebbins, the school janitor, if he would hunt up two wooden boxes about 18 inches square that might work as goals.

History has recorded several variations of this story, but their general conversation went something like this:

''Mr. Stebbins, I'm sorry to bother you, but I've been trying to invent a new game for a couple of weeks now and I'm just about to get it right.

''What I'm looking for is a pair of wooden boxes, say 18 inches across, into which the lads could toss a soccer ball.''

''Jeez, Doc, I don't know. Do you think the game will ever get off the ground?''

"That's my hope, Mr. Stebbins. Would there be any such boxes around? I know you're always putting them away in the basement."

"I'll tell you what, Doc, I don't have any wooden boxes right now, but I think I can find a pair of peach baskets. Would they work?"

And Stebbins — instantly claiming a clean corner in the janitorial Hall of Fame — returned with a pair of peach baskets.

That was the most timely substitution in the history of sport. Had Stebbins returned with two boxes, basketball would have become a round peg in a square basket. The ball would have bounded away at all angles. None of us would ever see the ball swirl tantalizingly around the rim, then drop in. Or fall out.

Wooden boxes would surely have sent The Doc back to the drawing board one more time, or maybe caused him to quit in disgust.

But the fates had even one more curtain call on that star-kissed December day. Naismith, peach baskets in hand, grabbed a hammer and nails and went into the tiny basement gymnasium to nail them to the overhead running track — a track that happened to be ten feet off the floor.

So add that to your list of peach basket miracles; the ten-foot basket, the goal to which Michael Jordan ascends with such amazing grace, the scene of 10,000 awe-inspring, in-your-face, reverse, double-pumping, slam-jamming dunks, is at that height only because the YMCA running track was ten feet off the floor.

It could have just as easily been 12 feet, or even 15.

So Naismith nailed up his peach baskets and, the really difficult work completed, went back to his office and wrote the original 13 rules of the game in less than an hour.

Miss Lyons, the school secretary, typed them on two sheets of paper and Naismith, with only a few minutes to spare on the 14th and final day, posted them on a bulletin board near the gym entrance.

Leonardo DaVinci should have had days like that!

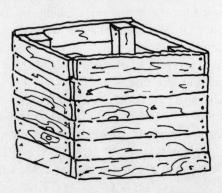

It could have been boxball.

Springfield Student

Springfield, MA. **Wednesday, April 1, 1987 No. 21**

James Naismith

Found To Be A Fraud

Jimmy Naismith: World renowned educator, innovator, and inventer of basketball, recently discovered to have been a lonely, homesick boy who despised hoops. (Photo by Pole Er Oid)

By B. Reel

James Naismith, believed to have founded basketball at Springfield College some 96 years ago, was really a lonely, depressed English major who had no interest in athletics, it was announced today by Dr. Edward S. Steitz, Athletic Director at Springfield College.

"Through our records, we've recently discovered that James Naismith did not, in fact, invent basketball, and to tell you the truth, he probably could've cared less for the sport," said Steitz.

The news came as a shock to the college, as plans for a celebration commemorating the 100th anniversary of the founding of the sport are already underway. In addition, plans for a Naismith statue to be located in front of the P.E. Complex are nearly finalized.

"We really don't know what to do. The statue has already been completed, and it was to be shipped to SC tomorrow. Maybe now we'll get a statue of Spuds McKenzie instead," said Dr. Frank S. Falcone, President of the college.

According to Falcone, Naismith was a lonely, "manic depressive kind of person" who was homesick and yearned to travel back to his family in Kansas. He kept to himself and rarely left his room in Alumni Hall. However, said Falcone, he did frequent Sass on Thursday nights and was a favorite of the bouncers there.

Evidently, he showed no interest in athletics and never played basketball, despite the constant nagging of his roommate to play a game of "one-on-one."

The startling news has forced basketball personnel across the country to ask "who did invent basketball?" No one seems to know for sure, but Steitz proposes that it could have been Naismith's roommate who invented the game on this campus in 1891.

April Fool edition of the "Springfield Student."

Chapter 3
THE IRON RIM
AND OTHER INVENTIONS
Amazing equipment

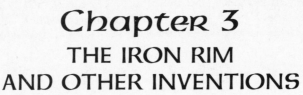
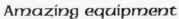

The appearance of the peach basket in the steady march of basketball progress was as brief as it was storied. The peach basket was too frail. Its size varied from state to state, depending on the whim of the local peach merchants. The angle of its opening was always dependent on the shape of the local gymnasium's balcony.

In 1892 Lew Allen of nearby Hartford, Connecticut, suggested replacing the peach basket with a cylindrical basket of heavy woven wire. Allen shaped his basket by bending a piece of the wire into a cylinder about 18 inches across and running a few cords across the bottom to keep the ball from falling out.

For some reason the early pioneers of the game steadfastly refused to let gravity take its full course. Each time a basket was made the ball had to be retrieved by poking it out with a long pole shoved through the bottom of the basket, or sending some faithful janitor like Pop Stebbins in search of a ladder.

Some help did arrive in 1893 when the Narragansett Machine Co. of Providence, Rhode Island, manufactured a goal with an iron rim, a cord basket, and a pulley and chain so the basket could be tipped like an old-fashioned flush toilet. According to advertisements of the day, the Narragansett basket was made of "strong iron hoops, with braided cord netting, arranged to be secured to a gymnasium gallery or wall for indoor use, or on an upright pipe, the bottom of which is spiked to be driven into the ground for outdoor use. By means of a cord the ball is easily discharged after a goal is made."

By 1906 some campus radicals were experimenting with nets that actually allowed the ball to drop through, but it wasn't until the 1913-14 season that it became legal to leave the bottom of the nets open.

In the mid-1930s the National Association of Basketball Coaches briefly experimented with expanding the rim from 18 to 20 inches, the better to hit the outside shots. The tests were conducted from 1936 to 1939 at the University of Missouri — deep in the heart of the "Show Me" state — but the experiment died right there.

American ingenuity took a large step for mankind in 1937 with the invention of a Rube Goldberg device called the Bask-o-Lite. The invention, which in some ways anticipated the modern era of basketball, was a goal with a little lever stretched across the opening below the net. When the ball dropped through, it would trigger a light behind the basket, verifying a goal. The Bask-o-Lite soon went the way of the hand-cranked telephone.

Still another early proposal — and this one is still popping up from time to time — was to raise the basket from 10 to 12 feet to cut down the effec-

An early basketball.

tiveness of the big man. The 12-foot goal was used in 1934 in an experimental game between the University of Kansas and Kansas State. Afterward, democracy reared its ugly head as the spectators voted three to one to keep the goal at The Doc's original 10 feet.

Subsequent experiments have proven, as always, that raising the goal actually gives the big man an even greater advantage; he is still the closest guy to the rim.

The backboard has also changed over the years. The earlier models, often made of wood, gave way to metal screens, partly because metal screening was lighter and was more easily adapted to portable, outdoor goals. The screens, however, would eventually develop deep dents that home teams could use to their advantage on bank shots. The smaller, fan-shaped, plate-glass backboards, cheaper and easier to use, were first authorized for the 1940-41 season. The rules of 1942-43 required a target to be painted on all transparent backboards, preferably a "square."

The trials of developing a basket with an automatic ball return and a dent-free backboard were minor compared to the larger matter of securing the perfectly round basketball.

The game had moved along for two years with a soccer ball as its principal weapon. Then, during the 1893-94 season, the Overman Wheel Company, a bicycle manufacturing firm, developed a new and larger ball with a circumference of between 30 and 32 inches. This size is reasonably close to the 30-inch standard of today.

The basketball history books don't say why a larger ball was needed, or why the task ended up in the hands of a wheel company. Perhaps Naismith's men found the soccer ball a little too small to shoot with two hands, and equally hard to dribble.

In any event, the very early rules said: "The only 'official' ball is made by the Overman Wheel Company, Chicopee Falls, Massachusetts. This ball has been adopted by the Association Athletic League, and must be used in all league games. Every ball is weighed, measured and tested by Dr. Luther Gulick as secretary of the league, and then stamped with his name. It is important that all associations use this ball, for otherwise there can be no guarantee of uniformity . . ."

Uniformity? There was more uniformity in Luther Gulick's pumpkin patch than there was with the early basketball. Those early creations were made by first sewing together, wrong-side out, four odd-shaped panels of tanned cowhide that had been glued to heavy canvas. Then the cowhide was turned right-side out and a rubber bladder with a protruding nipple was shoved through an opening in the cowhide. Finally, the bladder was inflated and the opening was laced shut with rawhide strips.

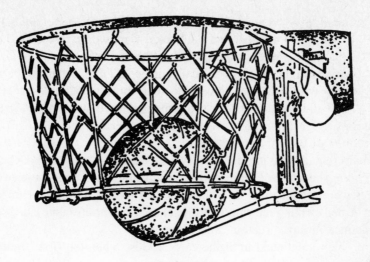

Bask-o-Lite.

The Spalding "Official" Basket Ball

Officially adopted and must be used in all match games. The cover is made in eight sections, with capless ends and of the finest and most carefully selected pebble grain leather. The bladder is made specially for this ball, of extra quality Para rubber. Each ball packed, complete, in sealed box, and guaranteed perfect in every detail.

The Spalding "Official" Basket Ball.
No. M. Each, **$5.00**

Extra Bladders
No. OM. For above. Each, **$1.25**

From the 1901 Spalding publication, "Basketball for Women."

The resultant product was often so lopsided that early basketball players, called "throwers" in the instructional books, were warned to grasp the ball in exactly the same way each time so . . . "the hands become familiar with any peculiarities in the shape of the ball, they adapt themselves to it and the ball is thrown with better judgment and with more chance of success."

By 1896-97 all basketball rules were being published by the A. G. Spalding Company, so, not surprisingly, A. G. Spalding became the only "official" manufacturer of basketballs.

The balls remained so inferior that few lasted a whole game without becoming pumpkin-shaped, or even oblong. Because the good ones were so rare, practices were often held with basketballs that looked more like Hungarian squash. A ball striking the rim, or the backboard, with its hand-laced seams could bounce in any direction, and often did.

The problem continued until the early 1930s, when the first "molded" basketballs were invented. They were not only cheaper, which made the game more accessible, but gave the dribbler some assurance the ball would return from the floor. Yet it wasn't until the 1949-50 season that the molded ball became the "official" ball.

The basketball also changed colors even before George Mikan and his American Basketball Association introduced the patriotic red, white and blue variety. In 1957 the national rules committee, realizing there was no official "color" for a basketball and a home team could play with a chartreuse ball if it so demanded, decreed that only a natural tan ball could be used. The one exception, if both teams agreed, was the use of a yellow-colored ball, because yellow had been found to be the best color for television purposes. One high school league did use a yellow ball for a time. In Hollywood.

Indications of just how rough basketball was in its early days can be seen in equipment advertisements of the early 1900s. One showed waist-to-calf "basketball pants" with almost as much padding as football pants of the day.

Left: Concealed lace basketball — 1927. Middle: Naismith seam-laced basketball — 1935. Right: Molded basketball. Leather panels sealed to a perfect spherical carcass. Special channeled seams allow better handling — 1941. Courtesy of Rawlings Sporting Goods Co.

Top left: Basketball pants, 1906. Note design and padding which resembles that of football pants used at this time. Bottom left: Official basketball goal and net, 1916. Catalog copy at that date mentioned that "bottom of net can be left open or, for match games, it can be closed by means of drawstring." Top right: What the well-dressed basketball player wore in 1922-1923. Courtesy of Rawlings Sporting Goods Co.

Another advertisement from the 1920s portrayed the well-equipped cager wearing a sleeveless worsted shirt, elbow pads, flannel knee pants, knee pads, thigh-high stockings, detachable hip pads and heavy basketball shoes with pure gum rubber soles. Legions of medieval knights went forth in search of dragons with less armor.

AMAZING ADVANCES IN EQUIPMENT

Basketball science moved ahead in 1973 when Ken Hayden of Avon, Ohio, invented a gadget called the "Reboundome." The device was an oddly-shaped plastic lid that fit over the basket. It was to be used by coaches as a rebounding aid if they were lucky enough to have players who never missed.

An Indiana high school coach, Virgil Sweet of Valparaiso, was actually given a patent (No. 3,629,869) for special glasses that prevented a player from looking down while dribbling. Not only would it improve ball-handling, but a player could learn to read an eye chart while on the move.

Chapter 4
THE DOC KEEPS
IT SIMPLE
Thirteen amazing rules
that changed America

The Original 13 Rules of Basketball, which appeared in the Springfield school newspaper, *The Triangle,* shortly after The Doc wrote them, indicated that Naismith was still a little uncertain if boxes or peach baskets were the best answer.

He was, of course, blissfully unaware of the wonderful monster he had just created. All he had wanted was a very simple game that would require a minimum amount of equipment, one that could be played with little notice, indoors or out, among any group that happened to have a peach basket, a balcony or a utility pole handy.

As you read the rules, you will also see The Doc was desperately trying to avoid mayhem, and yet had an almost eerie anticipation of some of the modern-day problems that lurked ahead.

You will also hear loud echoes of other games of his day, such as soccer, rugby and lacrosse. The more persistent echoes will remind you of girls' high school basketball as it is still played in Iowa, six on a side.

As a preface to his 13 rules, Naismith wrote: "The goals are a couple of baskets or boxes about 15 inches in diameter across the opening, and about 15 inches deep. These are suspended, one at each end of the grounds, about ten feet above the floor. The object of the game is to put the ball into your opponent's goal. This may be done by throwing the ball from any part of the grounds, with one or both hands."

The Doc also stipulated the ball was to be an "ordinary association ball," which in those days meant a soccer ball (or foot ball, as they called it).

He then listed the original 13 conditions and rules under which the game should be played.

"1. The ball may be thrown in any direction with one or both hands.

"2. The ball may be batted in any direction with one or both hands (never with the fist).

Opposite page: game and equipment as used in 1892. (From lecture material of Amos Alonzo Stagg.)

The Reach
Regulation Basket Ball

is made of fine Pebble Grain Cow-Hide Leather in six sections. Guaranteed perfect shape. Put up complete with Pure Para Rubber Bladder, Lacing Needle and Leather Lace.

No. 1½   Each   **$4.50**

The Reach
Special Basket Ball

is made of Selected Pebble Grain Sheepskin Leather in eight sections. Put up complete with Pure Para Rubber Bladder and Lace.

No. 2   Each   **$3.00**

The Reach
Practice Basket Ball

is made of fine Brown Grain Sheepskin Leather, with capped ends. Put up complete with Pure Para Rubber Bladder and Lace.

No. 3   Each   **$2.00**

The Value of the Reach Trade Mark is that it Insures a Return of One Hundred Cents for Every Dollar Spent

Basketballs from an early Reach catalog.

Style of official basketball used during the early years of the game. Note lace construction.

"3. A player cannot run with the ball. The player must throw it from the spot on which he catches it, allowance to be made for a man who catches the ball at a good speed if he tries to stop.

"4. The ball must be held in or between the hands. The arms or body must not be used for holding it.

"5. No shouldering, holding, pushing, tripping, or striking in any way the person of an opponent shall be allowed; the first infringement of this by any player shall count as a foul, the second shall disqualify him until the next goal is made, or, if there was evident intent to injure the player, for the whole of the game, no substitute allowed.

"6. A foul is striking at the ball with the fist, violation of Rules 3, 4 and such as described in Rule 5.

"7. If either side makes three consecutive fouls, it shall count as a goal for the opponents (consecutive means without the opponents in the meantime making a foul).

"8. A goal shall be made when the ball is thrown or batted from the ground into the basket and stays there, providing those defending the goal do not touch or disturb the goal. If the ball rests on the edges and the opponents move the basket, it shall count as a goal.

"9. When the ball goes out of bounds it shall be thrown into the field of play by the person first touching it. In case of a dispute, the umpire shall throw it straight into the field. The thrower-in is allowed five seconds, if he holds it longer, it shall go to the opponent. If any side persists in delaying the game, the umpire shall call a foul on that side.

"10. The umpire shall be the judge of men and shall note the fouls and notify the referee when three consecutive fouls have been made. He shall have the power to disqualify men according to Rule 5.

"11. The referee shall be the judge of the ball and shall decide when the ball is in play, in bounds, to which side it belongs, and shall keep time. He shall decide when a goal has been made, and keep account of the goals with any other duties that are usually performed by a referee.

"12. The time shall be 15 minute halves, with five minutes rest between.

"13. The side making the most goals in that time shall be declared the winner. In case of a draw, the game may, by agreement of the captains, be continued until another goal is made."

That was it, sports fans, the 13 basic rules that forever changed how America would spend its winters. Still grasping for the proper ground rules, Naismith also added a few more thoughts on his general concept and philosophy of the game.

He wrote:

"The number composing a team depends largely on the size of the floor space, but it may range from three on a side to forty. The fewer players down to three, the more scientific it may be made, but the more players, the more fun.

"The men may be arranged according to the idea of the captain, but it has been found that a goal keeper, two guards, three center men, two wings and a home man stationed in above order from the goal is best.

"It shall be the duty of the goal keeper and the two guards to prevent the opponent from scoring. The duty of the wing men and the home man is to put the ball in the opponent's goal, and the center shall feed the ball forward to the man who has the best opportunity, thus nine men make the best number for a team."

There was a very good reason why Naismith thought nine men on a side would be a great way to play basketball: the class he was teaching at the training school had 18 students.

So history was made sometime in late December, 1891, when Naismith divided his class into two teams, chose a center from each side and then tossed the ball up between them — the latter a quaint custom that's lasted about 100 years.

The 18 players were crowded into a dim, cluttered basement gymnasium with a playing surface about 35 feet wide and 50 feet long. Most wore the gym uniform of the day, long gray pants and short-sleeved jerseys. Due to a lack of qualified personnel, The Doc served as both umpire and referee in that game.

Because the bottoms had been left in the peach baskets, which had been nailed to the balcony at a rather rakish angle, the ever-resourceful "Pop" Stebbins was on hand with a stepladder to retrieve any successful shots.

The history books say there was only one; a student named William R. Chase dropped in a shot from near mid court — which was only about 25 feet — to score the first basket in the history of the game.

February, 12, 1892

There will be a contest between the athletes of the central and Hill branches of the Young Men's Christian association at the Armory Hill gymnasium to-night. The sport is the new-fangled game of "basket ball," an indoor substitute for football invented by Mr Naismith of the training school. The game is played by nine men on each side, and the object is to get the ball into the enemy's basket, which is suspended in the air at the goal. There is considerable scope for activity and for hard work, and the young men get a good deal of sport out of it. It is thought that it will be introduced generally into the Young Men's Christian association gymnasiums of the country. It is one of the few indoor games that are valuable for exercise as well for amusemer .

The basket-ball game between the boys' department of the Armory Hill branch and the boys' department of the central branch of the Young Men's Christian association, played in the Armory Hill gymnasium last night resulted in a tie, the score being 2—2. About 100 spectators were present to witness the game, which proved so interesting that arrangements will soon be made to play off the tie. The game is a very pretty one to watch. At each end of the floor is a narrow, deep basket, suspended against the gallery. The game is played with an ordinary association ball and the object is to throw it into the enemy's basket, the enemy in the meantime doing everything possible to prevent that result. Each "pocket" counts one, and in most games the score runs up to 10 or 15, so that the match last night was an unusually hard-fought one.

March 12, 1892

BASKET FOOTBALL GAME.

Over 200 spectators craned their necks over the gallery railing of the Christian workers' gymnasium while they watched the game of "basket ball" yesterday afternoon between the teachers of the International Young Men's Christian association training school and the students. The teams were as follows: Teachers, Gulick, Clark, Naismith, Stagg, Morse, Bown and Myer; students, Davis, Mahn, Thompson, Archibald, Ruggles, Libby and McDonald. The teachers worked hard and performed wonders of agility and strength, but they were not "in it" with the students, who had the advantage in science, and the score at the end was 5—1 in favor of the latter. The most conspicuous figure on the floor was Stagg in the blue Yale uniform, who managed to have a hand in every scrimmage. His football training hampered him, and he was perpetually making fouls by shoving his opponents. He managed, however, to score the only goal that the instructors made. Dr Gulick and Dr Clark also did good work for their side. Among the stu-

dents the best work was done by Ruggles, who tossed the ball into the illusive basket four times, and McDonald who scored once and did a great deal of brilliant playing. The spectators followed the game with much interest and amusement. Another game will be played soon between the seniors and the faculty of the physical department. The tie game between the boys of the Hill and the town association will be played off Tuesday evening.

March 19, 1892

STAGG'S LECTURE ON ATHLETICS.

A fairly large audience gathered in City hall last evening to hear the lecture on "The Modern Athlete" by one of the most popular of them, Alonzo Stagg, the pitcher and football player. The stereopticon pictures, which furnished the staple of the entertainment, were preceded by a rapid sketch of the history of athletics from the time that Adam was caught napping and was put out down to the present day.

Amos Alonzo Stagg.

March 16, 1892

About 250 people attended the game of basket ball between the Armory Hill and main Young Men's Christian associations last evening at the Armory Hill gymnasium. The Hill boys beat by a score of 1 to 0.

The Aztec game of Ollamalitzli.

FIVE MORE AMAZING FACTS ABOUT
EARLY BASKETBALL

★ A skeptical student named Frank Mahon was one of the two captains in Naismith's first basketball scrimmage. He came to like the game, and first suggested to The Doc that it be named "Naismith ball." The Doc, ever humble, declined. So Mahon then suggested it be called, oddly enough, basket ball — with two words. The Doc said fine.

★ The Doc eventually confessed he only played basketball twice in his life; the first time a few weeks after he invented it, and the second time about seven years later when he was working at the University of Kansas.

★ Some anthropologists and archaeologists report that Naismith may not have invented basketball after all; there's evidence that ball-and-hoop games were played in Mexico in the 10th century B.C. and among the Mayan Indians of Yucatan in the year 900.

Also, the 16th century Aztecs played a particularly tough brand of ball and hoop called Ollamalitzli. The player who made a shot was entitled to the clothing of all the spectators; the captain of the losing team often had his head chopped off.

★ As father of the game, Naismith was in charge of all its rules for the next two years. His first book, *Rules for Basket Ball,* was published in 1892 by the Springfield Printing and Binding Co.

★ In its early days basketball was often called "basket football," or "football in a gym." A half-period was called an "inning" and a goal was called a "touchdown."

The Reach
Basket Ball Bladders

are made of **Pure Para Rubber** and thoroly tested by the manufacturers and ourselves, and in addition to this we guarantee them. See Page 5 for guarantee.

Each

No. **OH** For Basket Balls No. 0 . . . . . **$2.00**

No. **OA** For Basket Balls Nos. 1X and 1½ . **1.50**

No. **5B** For Basket Balls Nos. 2, 3 and 4B **1.00**

Four Piece Nos. OH–OA

Two Piece No. 5B

Bladders from an early Reach catalog.

37

Chapter 5
NINE'S FINE FOR BASEBALL, BUT . . .
Amazing Rule changes

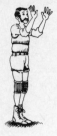

ASKET BALL

OUTFITS.

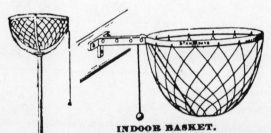

INDOOR BASKET.

The baskets are strong iron hoops, with braided cord netting, arranged to be secured to a gymnasium gallery or wall for indoor use, or on an upright pipe the bottom of which is spiked to be driven into the ground for outdoor use. By means of a cord the ball is easily discharged after a goal is made.

Indoor Goals, per pair,	$15.00
Outdoor Goals, per pair,	30.00
No 10 Association Foot Ball, each,	3.25
American Rubber Foot Ball,	1.25

Prices for Special Portable Baskets for Exhibitions in Halls or low priced outfits given on application.

OUTDOOR BASKET.

Narragansett Machine Co.
Gymnasium Outfitters. Providence, R. I.

Time Marches on — 1893. To release the ball, you merely pull the chain.

If The Doc didn't soon realize it, the rest of the world did: nine on a side was too many for basketball. However, such numbers had not slowed the game's amazing growth. A November 12, 1893, story in *The New York Times* said basketball was already being played coast to coast in the United States and had made beachheads in Japan, England and Australia.

Most of the international growth had come from Christian missionaries. They learned the game at Naismith's shoes in Springfield, and then took it around the world. But the rules varied greatly from place to place. The same *Times* article described a game — later the norm in women's basketball — in which the courts were divided into three equal sections, with three players assigned to each section.

Basically, the back three players handled the defense, the middle three advanced the ball, and the three nearest the opponent's goal, one of them called a "home man," had all the fun; they got to shoot.

The Doc, of course, hadn't been able to cover everything in his original 13 rules. The game evolved too quickly; in fact, we are still changing the rules almost 100 years later.

Naismith and Gulick did combine on a new rules book in 1894. But then Naismith drifted away from all the rules problems to go on to other things. For a time after than, Gulick was the Godfather of the Rule Book. Then the basketball pioneers did what all men do in times of crisis: they formed committees to work on the rules.

What follows is a chronology taken from *The New York Times*, of the rule and equipment changes made in the early years of basketball, as its leaders struggled to give it some sense and continuity.

Most are long forgotten. Many were just as cussed and discussed as the three-point shot is today.

The Reach "Official" Basket Ball Guide

The best we have ever issued; contains photographs of all the leading clubs throughout the United States with complete records—new rules--also full instructions how to score. Edited by Wm. J. Scheffer, one of the best authorities in the United States on this great game.

Price, 10 Cents

The Reach "Official" Basket Ball Score Book

is made with Cloth Cover, contains enough pages to score 25 games, has full instructions how to score.

Price, 25 Cents

39

1896

Not only was the invention of basketball something of a happy accident, but so was the creation of the backboard. Backboards were not first hung up behind the basket as an aid to scoring; they became necessary because too many overwrought fans in the balcony — some armed with umbrellas — were reaching out and knocking the shots away from the baskets.

Naismith, of course, hadn't given much thought to "umbrellatending." But the only way to stop it was to place a big, flat hunk of wood behind the basket. The eventual use of this piece of wood to help a shot carom into the goal was secondary.

The first backboards were 6 feet tall and 12 feet wide and probably blotted out the sun (wood must have been a lot cheaper then).

Metal screening was also used as backboard material for a time, then smaller pieces of wood, and, still later, 4 foot by 6 foot hunks of glass.

Then came Darryl Dawkins and everybody thought maybe wood wasn't such a bad idea after all.

1900

The basketball committee of the Amateur Athletic Union, which had been created in 1896 to help Gulick with the rules, added to Rule 11, Section 1, an addendum that said "the ball must enter and remain in the basket until after the referee's decision of said goal."

That was considered necessary because by then the bottom was being cut out of some peach baskets to allow the ball to drop through. Alas, sometimes the ball went through so quickly the spectators could not tell if a goal had been scored. No one had yet invented the basketball net, so the bottoms were ordered back on the baskets.

In 1900, the dribble, which Naismith hadn't even considered in his original rules, was also proving troublesome. So in that same meeting the basketball committee decided a player could only dribble once, and then with both hands, before having to toss the ball to another player.

Talk of anticipating problems: the rules committee also decided that year that a goal made from out of bounds must not count.

The Amateur Athletic Union and college basketball officials met in the Hotel Imperial in New York, where they decided to maintain their separate rules for the game.

This was done because the college game — with more emphasis on the dribble instead of merely passing the ball — was considered much too tough and strenuous to be adapted for use in athletic clubs and YMCAs. The game was still considered social exercise in the YMCAs; the college men said they did not want such a ''less vigorous game.''

A committee was appointed, however, to add definite restrictions against rough play, to order disqualification for obvious offenses, and to clearly define all fouls.

Testament to some need for a rules change had come a few months earlier while Yale was pulverizing Harvard 27 to 6 and Captain Burnham of Harvard was whistled for 15 fouls.

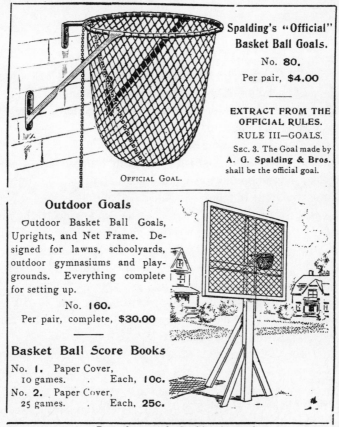

Spalding's "Official" Basket Ball Goals.

No. **80.**

Per pair, **$4.00**

EXTRACT FROM THE OFFICIAL RULES.

RULE III—GOALS.

SEC. 3. The Goal made by **A. G. Spalding & Bros.** shall be the official goal.

OFFICIAL GOAL.

Outdoor Goals

Outdoor Basket Ball Goals, Uprights, and Net Frame. Designed for lawns, schoolyards, outdoor gymnasiums and playgrounds. Everything complete for setting up.

No. **160.**

Per pair, complete, **$30.00**

Basket Ball Score Books

No. **1.** Paper Cover,
10 games. . Each, **10c.**
No. **2.** Paper Cover,
25 games. . Each, **25c.**

Page from early Spalding's catalog.

1908

The recently formed Collegiate Basket Ball Rules Committee, trying to curb the rough play that plagued college basketball, added a second official to call the games. Until then only one referee had been used. And used. And used.

The same committee also finally defined the dribble as the "continuous passage of the ball." That, for the first time, stopped college players from being able to start a dribble, stop it, then start it again — your classic double, triple or even quadruple dribble.

The rule makers also decided that it would be legal for a player to take a shot after completing a dribble. Prior to that, players had to pass the ball when their dribble was completed and let someone else get all the glory.

Finally, although the article made no specific mention of the feared Captain Burnham, the committee decided any player who committed five fouls should go to the pines.

1910

OK, the feared Captain Burnham has been maligned a little unfairly. In the early days of basketball, ANY offense such as running with the ball, illegally striking the ball or a double dribble was considered a foul. Captain Burnham may just have been a lousy ball handler.

But the Intercollegiate Basket Ball Rules Committee attempted to rectify this problem by decreeing any person committing four personal fouls should be disqualified. The good news was the fouls had to be of a more flagrant nature such as holding, blocking, pushing or tripping.

While this sounds like the rules committee had anticipated Bobby Knight's "No Blood-No Pick" style coaching, that was not entirely true. In fact, the rules committee didn't anticipate that there would be coaching at all, at least not during actual games. The committee decided that, "There shall be no coaching during the progress of the game by anybody connected with either of the teams. For the violation of this the offending side shall be warned once by the referee, and if the offense is repeated the opposing team shall be given a free throw for the basket."

Can you believe it? No game coaching! How pure could a game get?

1914

The same rules committee met in the Hotel Astor in New York, this time to discuss the possibility of allowing a player to return to the game once he had been taken out.

Until then, once a player was removed from the game he might as well go wait in the trolley car. The result was the starters would often stay in the game the whole time. The only way out was death, four personal fouls or any combination of the two.

Some coaches, claiming visiting teams could not afford to take more than eight players on the road, complained the new rule would give the home team an unfair advantage.

1915

For the first time since Naismith tacked up his peach baskets, the rules for the YMCA, AAU and college games were made the same.

This was really a major step in the popularity of basketball. Until then the irreconcilable difference had been that troublesome dribble; the YMCA and AAU players were not permitted a shot after a dribble, supposedly because it discouraged teamwork and made the game rougher.

The collegians had been firing away after the dribble since 1908.

1920

A mere six years after the matter was first discussed, the rules committee for the Intercollegiate Basketball League decided it would be fine for a player to go in and out of a game once, provided he hadn't committed four fouls.

Road trips have never been the same.

The amazing Billy Barty demonstrates one rule of basketball that will never change; there will always be a place for the quick little man in basketball.

1923

Here's another one you may not believe: The joint rules committee of the Intercollegiate Basketball League decided that the designated free throw shooter — the DFTS, if you will — would no longer be allowed to shoot foul shots for each team.

Prior to that rule change, and about 40 years too early for Wilt Chamberlain, teams were allowed to have one hot-shot foul shooter attempt all free throws.

From that point on, the person fouled had to be the one stepping nervously to the free throw line.

The rules committee maintained the new rule would make the game more even because everybody would have to practice free throws.

In a way, the new rule was like asking the guy who scored the touchdown to kick the extra point. Its long-range effect has been to add a half-hour to every basketball practice and condemn millions of poor-shooting high school kids to a late, cold supper.

1928

You'd think that by 1928 the problems with the dribble would have been solved, but it remained the source of great argument.

The complaint was that dribbles were taking over the game. From Day One basketball had been envisioned as a quiet sport featuring great passing and teamwork, and here were these ball hogs dribbling all over the place crashing into people.

So maybe things haven't changed so much in 60 years.

The controversy grew so strong that in 1927 dribblers were limited to just one bounce. That restriction, of course, didn't satisfy anyone, and this rule met a merciful death the next year.

So to check the dribbler (and this was also a controversial move in its day), the rules committee said that any dribbler who charged into an opponent would be called for a foul.

It makes you wonder what kind of contact was allowed before that.

1932

In spite of all efforts to speed up the game, there were still many teams in the early 1930s that preferred to go with a four-corner offense for 40 minutes. Perpetual stalling was in vogue, and it made for some mighty dull games. So the rules people got together and invented the ten-second line.

Only they called it, naturally, the "centre line."

They made this center line exactly two inches wide, and said if a team didn't get the ball across it in ten seconds it would be a turnover.

But the rules people still weren't willing to go all the way to end stalling. They also said that if the offensive team regained possession of the ball after a shot, it could throw it back over the ten-second line "but once," and start over.

That, of course, would be today's over-and-back.

Another change made in 1932 was to prohibit a player with the ball from spending more than three seconds in the free-thow lane. Prior to that the big men could stand in the lane waving the ball aloft like a pompom for as long as they liked.

But a man without the ball could still stand in there all night.

1933

Basketball remained badly divided in the early 1930s. In one corner there was the National Collegiate Athletic Association (NCAA) and the many high school federations. In the other corner dribbled the Amateur Athletic Union (AAU) and the many YMCAs.

However, even the colleges couldn't agree on all the rules. Since the game's early days, there had been a jump ball after every basket. In 1933, to speed up play, some of the West Coast schools had already eliminated a center jump after each basket and were allowing the opponents to take the ball out of bounds.

The East Coast stayed with the center jump after every basket, allowing the team with the big center to pretty much control the game.

An attempt to end these geographic differences was made in April, 1933, during an experimental all-star game in New York. The game started with the traditional center jump, but after each basket the teams ALTERNATED taking the ball out of bounds — from the center line.

News reports indicated the skeptics didn't think that would work either.

1935

Finally, some progress: in April, 1935, the National Basketball Committee of the United States and Canada decided that after a successful free throw the team scored upon would put the ball in play at the end of the court where the goal had been made.

Just as important, the committee also decided no offensive player would be allowed to stay in the lane more than three seconds with or without the ball.

That was a monumental change. Basketball had been more and more dominated by the big men who would camp inside; the free throw line had begun to look like four dwarfs attacking a Maypole.

Another change allowed a basket to count if a player was fouled in the act of shooting. This, finally, prevented the defensive player from shoving the offensive player into the water bucket on every shot.

Now basketball was really rolling.

1937

Well, not entirely rolling. It wasn't until 1937 that the center jump after every basket was dropped!

The committee also decided the ball should be put back in play under the opponent's basket after every free throw or goal.

Now basketball was really, really rolling.

THE AMAZING HISTORY OF THE THREE-POINT SHOT

The fabled, and cursed, three-point shot has never stayed in one place very long. Early basketball was partly modeled after football, so the first basketball "field goals" were worth three points. They became two points shortly afterward.

The three-point shot reappeared in 1962 with Abe Saperstein and his short-lived American Basketball League. The ABL — actually Saperstein — decreed any shot from more than 25 feet was worth three points, and it probably should have been. Since the first ABL game was played at Oakland between the Kansas City Steers and the Oakland Oaks on November 14, 1962, it's safe to assume the first modern three-point shot was hoisted there.

When the American Basketball Association began in the mid 1960s it also used the three-point shot. The immortal Les Selvage of the Anaheim Amigos made history in 1968 by launching an amazing 26 three-point shots in one game, a record few dared to challenge. He made 10.

The older, wiser, duller National Basketball Association treated the three-point shot as a gimmick until the 1979-80 season. Then the NBA adopted it — from behind a line 23-feet 9-inches at the top of the key and 22 feet in the corners.

The NBA record for three-point shots in one game is 11 set by Darrell Griffith of the Utah Jazz against Houston on April 26, 1985. He made five, which tied the NBA record for most three-pointers made in a game.

After much trial and error, the three-point shot, from 19-feet 9-inches, was adopted for men's college basketball for the 1986-87 season. The women adopted it for the 1987-88 season, as will most high school teams.

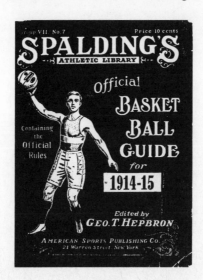

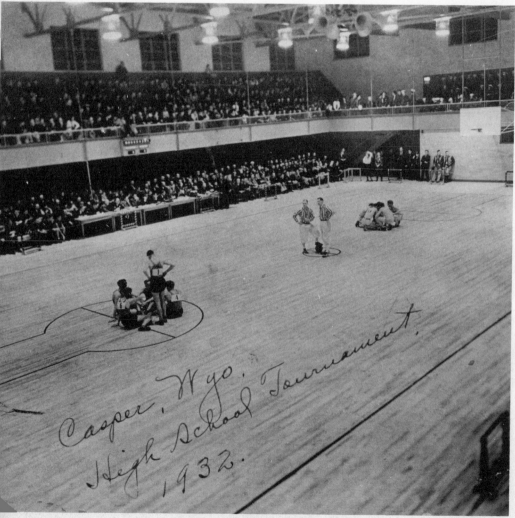

Notice how the teams huddled on the floor long ago.

College basketball is riding a huge popularity wave. Professional basketball, even though the season drags on like a bad marriage, is also gaining in favor, partly because of all the highly-publicized collegians moving into the game. Yet both are new kids on the block compared to our enduring love for high school basketball.

The high school game is for the home boys, and girls. It's for the kid down the street who's been heaving a basketball at a rickety garage hoop since he was old enough to spell Larry Bird. It's for the inner-city kids, who, far from the hum of the automatic garage-door opener, can still unite a whole town for one weekend in late March. Those are homegrown kids out there, and it makes all the emotional difference.

James Naismith said in his autobiography that "basketball was accepted by the high schools before the colleges took it up as an organized sport... I believe that the younger boys who played in the YMCA gymnasiums took the game with them into the high schools."

It wasn't uncommon in the early days for high school teams to beat college teams. There were no age restrictions and very few eligiblity requirements, so some high school "stars" hung around long enough to earn a pension.

Naismith said he knew of a basketball league being formed in Denver as early as 1896. In 1897 the Holyoke (Massachusetts) High School was playing a full schedule, and in 1900 it won an 11-team tournament in Boston.

Wisconsin, a state better known for its cows than basketball coaches, held the first state high school tournament in 1905. It was, like many of the early state tournaments, an invitational affair with the top teams in the Badger State invited to Lawrence College in Appleton to find a top gun. The winner, the first in an 80-year pageant of joy and tears, was Fond du Lac.

Illinois, Kansas and Utah began state tournaments in 1908; Louisiana and Ohio followed in 1909. By 1920, half the states in the country were holding state championships.

The problem was that many of these states held monster elimination tournaments at one site instead of the regional-playoff systems used today. In some states 150 teams and 1,500 players might converge on the same gymnasium for a showdown that would last slightly longer than the Boer War. Indiana was among the first states to spread the game over several sites, cutting down on travel while moving the excitement to a dozen locations.

Up until about 1960, many of the state championships were won by tiny schools with fair-sized gymnasiums and very large followings. Basketball was a small-town game. Almost every state had a legendary David, a team like Hebron in Illinois or Milan in Indiana that won state championships with male enrollments you could put in a phone booth. The recent hit movie "Hoosiers," in fact, was based on the 1954 "Miracle of Milan."

Party because many black teams were barred from state competition until the 1960s, it wasn't until modern times that the big-city schools began to capture more championships. Now many states (Indiana, Maryland and Kentucky among the exceptions) have gone to class tournaments based on school size. The Davids can still win state championships, but they're playing against other people named Dave.

The one team that best illustrates how bonkers people can be over high school basketball is a 1928 squad from deep in the hills of Kentucky — the Carr Creek Creekers.

In 1928 there were maybe 200 people living in Carr Creek and 15 students in its hillside school, eight of them boys. The school had no gymnasium; it had an auditorium with a 12-foot ceiling. Unless it rained or snowed, the team practiced outside.

The Creekers had no uniforms until they won a few regional games in Richmond. The locals were so impressed they passed the hat — or maybe the coonskin cap — collected $55 and bought Carr Creek new uniforms.

Suitably attired, Carr Creek won its first three games in the 1928 Kentucky State Tournament, but lost the championship to Ashland in a four-overtime thriller, 13-11.

That was only the beginning of the Carr Creek story. In those days of barnstorming high school teams, the National Interscholastic Tournament was held annually in Chicago. The tournament determined the national champion in high school basketball from 1917-1931. The Creekers, along with Ashland, were among the 40 teams invited in 1928.

Carr Creek not only became a Chicago favorite, but a national favorite. The wire services sent out 100,000 words about these ragamuffin mountain boys, and Will Rogers mentioned them in his syndicated column.

The Creekers' legend grew as they beat state championship teams from New Mexico and Texas, but the bubble burst when a team from Vienna, Georgia, sent them home, 22-11.

Ashland, incidentally, beat Vienna in the finals to claim the national championship, ending the season 37-0. In the next two years teams from tiny Athens, Texas, won the national championship, traveling north in cars and playing games along the way. By then, the national tournament had become so big and commercialized that the University of Chicago decided to end it.

Eight years earlier, in 1922, a most unusual game had been played in Chicago in that National Interscholastic Tournament, which involved another crowd favorite. The Lexington, Kentucky, Blue Devils and Cathedral High of Duluth, Minnesota, both arrived with blue jerseys. To eliminate the confusion, the University of Chicago loaned its maroon shirts, bearing the name Chicago, to the Blue Devils. The adopted Lexington squad earned the support of the Chicago crowd and won the tournament.

Carr Creek did win a Kentucky championship in 1956, but, giving way to progress, had to close its doors in 1974 to merge with a larger school.

There have been other highly-publicized high school teams. Between 1925 and 1929 Passaic (New Jersey) High School, playing for Professor Ernest A. Blood, won 159 consecutive games, over a stretch that included five straight undefeated seasons. Both are national boys' records. The Baskin, Louisiana, girls' team, however, did even better, winning 218 straight games between

This Carr Creek team captured the nation's fancy in 1928.

The all-time leading high school scorers: Greg Procell and Lynne Lorenzen.

1947 and 1953 as part of a string that included seven consecutive state championships.

In January, 1965, DeMatha High School defeated Power Memorial and Lew Alcindor 46-43 before 12,500 in one of the most famous high school games ever played. Power hadn't lost in almost three years before this defeat.

The all-time boys' record for scoring in a single game belongs to Danny Heater, a slim, aptly-named guard from Burnsville, West Virginia, who scored 135 points on January 26, 1960.

Doug Huff, sports editor of the Wheeling (West Virginia) *Intelligencer* and an avid high school historian, put together a history of that game.

He wrote that Heater's need for a college basketball scholarship coincided with the appearance of a thoroughly outmanned team from Widen, West Virginia, in Burnsville's 30- by 50-foot gymnasium.

In the first half Heater scored 53 of his team's 75 points. In the second half, with his teammates continually pressing and passing him the ball, Heater added another 82 points, including 55 in the final 10 minutes. When the game ended he'd made 53 of 70 field goal attempts and 29 of 41 free throws.

Heater, who averaged 27 points a game that season, won a basketball scholarship to the University of Richmond, but had to drop out of school to support his parents when their home was destroyed in a fire.

The girls' one-game record was set by Marie Boyd of Lonaconing Central, Maryland, who scored 156 points on February 24, 1924. The record, however, was set in an era when women played six or more to a team and only certain players could shoot. Boyd hit 77 baskets and two free throws in her team's thrilling 163-3 win over nearby Ursuline Academy.

The record book shows that 14 girls have scored over 100 in a game, but only Cheryl Miller, later a USC legend, scored more than 100 points in a regulation, five-on-five game. Miller, of Riverside Poly, California, scored 105 points against Riverside Norte Vista on January 26, 1982.

Greg Procell of tiny Noble Ebarb High School in Louisiana holds the all-time high school career scoring record compiled during his 181-game career between 1967 and 1970. He scored 3,173 points in his senior year, averaging 46.7 points a game for 68 games and 6,702 for his career.

The all-time leading girls' scorer is Lynne Lorenzen of Ventura, Iowa, who scored 6,736 points during a four-year varsity career of six-girl basketball. She scored 1,173 points her freshman year, 1,858 points her sophomore year, 1,770 points her junior year and 1,935 points her senior year. She averaged 60.1 points per game over her 112-game high school career with a shooting average of about 75 percent.

Other amazing point totals from Doug Huff's files are:

• Wilt Chamberlain of Philadelphia Overbrook High School scored 90 points in three quarters against Roxborough in 1955, then sat out the rest of the game.

• Billy Miller of Nancy, Kentucky, scored 50 points in one quarter in 1976.

• On January 27, 1918, Shinnston, West Virginia, shut out Weirton, West Virginia, 136 to 0.

• In 1923 a benevolent quintet from Kansas High of Kansas City eased past a team called the "Rainbows" 234-2, a record that still stands as a monument to sportsmanship.

• Daryl Moreau of New Orleans de LaSalle hit 126 consecutive free throws over 21 games in two seasons, ending in 1979.

1911 Crawfordsville team, the first Indiana state champions.

Here are some other amazing marks in the national high school record book (through the 1985-86 season).

BOYS' RECORDS

Career Points
6,702 Greg Procell, Noble Ebarb, Louisiana; 1967-70
5,367 Bruce Williams, Florien, Louisiana; 1977-80
5,030 Jackie Moreland, Linden, Louisiana; 1953-56
4,896 Bennie Fuller, Little Rock School for Deaf; 1968-71
4,337 King Kelly Coleman, Wayland, Kentucky; 1953-56.

Points Per Game/Single Season
54.0 Bobby Joe Douglas, Marion, Louisiana; 1979-80
53.7 Ervin Stepp, Phelps, Kentucky; 1979-80
50.9 Bennie Fuller, Little Rock School for Deaf; 1970-71
50.4 Kent Hyde, Onida, South Dakota; 1953-54
49.8 Steve Farquhar, Calvary Baptist Christian, New Jersey; 1984-85.

Career Rebounds
3,059 Bruce Williams, Florien, Louisiana; 1977-80
1,929 Rick Goodman, Belt Valley, Montana; 1968-71
1,593 Cliff Poindexter, Fresno, California; 1970-73.

Most Coaching Wins
1,026 Leslie Gaudet, Pine Prairie, Louisiana; 1937-42, 1947-70
 924 Eric Staples, Perry, Georgia; 1933-65
 923 Walter Vanhuss, four Tennessee schools; 1953-86
 896 Charles Womack, Hawley, Texas; 1947-79
 886 Ralph Tasker, Hobbs, New Mexico; 1940-86.

GIRLS' RECORDS

Career Points
6,736 Lynne Lorenzen, Ventura, Iowa; 1983-87
6,250 Denise Long, Union Whitten, Iowa; 1965-69
5,103 Debbie Coats, Mediapolis, Iowa; 1971-75
4,875 Sandra Fiete, Garnavillo, Iowa; 1950-55
4,798 Harriet Taylor, New Sharon, Iowa; 1953-57.

The 1928-29 Bristol High School team, which won several awards for uniform coordination.

Career Assists

1,078 Jonnah McDonnell, Marlboro Central, New York; 1981-84
  670 Tami Fick, Coronado, California; 1976-79
  612 Kellie Cardona, Alhambra, California; 1975-79.

Career Rebounds

1,634 Necie Thompson, Gahr, California; 1976-80
1,617 Cathy Snipes, Alton, Illinois; 1982-85
1,604 Cheryl Miller, Riverside Poly, California; 1979-82.

Most Coaching Wins

1,152 Bertha Teague, Ada Byng, Oklahoma; 1928-70
1,063 T. Hill, Hardy Highland, Arkansas; 1952-86
1,040 Jim Smiddy, Cleveland, Tennessee; 1949-86
  735 Galen Johnson, Maryville, Tennessee; 1952-79
  717 Wayne Merryman, three Oklahoma schools; 1956-86.

And just for the record, Charles Womack of Hawley, Texas, led his boys' teams to 896 wins and the girls' teams to 674 wins for a total of 1,570 wins at one school, an all-time, if not all-universe, record.

Chapter 7
SENDA BERENSEN
AND THE SMITH SISTERS
Women's basketball makes
an amazing debut

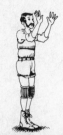

Barely one month after soccer ball first touched peach basket in the Springfield YMCA, a few women teachers from nearby Buckingham Grade School began dropping by on their way to lunch.

Basketball had begun in a gym in the YMCA basement. The famed balcony where the first peach basket was attached led to a ground-level door which the teachers passed.

They had heard the shouts in the gymnasium, stepped to the balcony door to see what the noise was all about, and stayed to watch and applaud this strange new game.

This was an era when men were men and women were supposed to play badminton, pat their fevered brows and faint when appropriate. Happily, these teachers were on the cutting edge of social progress; two weeks later they were asking The Doc for a little playing time of their own.

Naismith, of course, obliged.

He later wrote in his autobiography:

"When the time arrived, the girls appeared at the gymnasium, some with tennis shoes, but the majority with street shoes. None of them changed from their street clothes, costumes which were not made for freedom of movement. I shall never forget the sight that they presented in their long trailing dress with leg-of-mutton sleeves, and in several cases with the hint of a bustle."

Such was the first women's basketball game, or at least the first practice. One of those ladies in that magic winter of 1891-92 hoisted the first female shot of a game soon to be heard around the world, bustle or not.

Indeed, several of the teachers began practicing daily, developed some basic fundamentals, and two women's teams were formed at the YMCA.

In March, 1892, the YMCA men hosted a basketball tournament; it was only afterwards — as too often would be the case with women's basketball — that someone suggested that the women should also have a tournament.

One of those women was Maude Sherman, who would later marry James Naismith, thus completing one of the more unusual double plays in basketball history. She not only played in the first women's game, she married its inventor.

In 1893 the women's game spread to Smith College in nearby Northampton, Massachusetts. Senda Berensen, the director of physical education at the college, had learned about the game at a Yale seminar, talked with Naismith about it, and then taken it home to Northhampton.

The first women's collegiate game was played at Smith in 1893 between freshmen and sophomore teams. No males were allowed to watch because

Opposite page: Miss Senda Berensen, in long dress, with Smith College students in Northampton, Mass., where women played the first public basketball game March 22, 1893.

"Basketball . . . should be admitted only tentatively, and under professional supervision, to a place among the sports open to women of a new age . . . The chances of permanent injury to beauty and health, the evil influence of such excitement upon the emotional and nervous feminine nature, and the tendency to unsex the player, is not womanly . . . " Lucille Eaton Hill, Wellesley College, 1903.

Right: Senda Berensen. Below: 1894-95 team from New York and Massachusetts.

1897.

the players were wearing bloomers; the class of '96 cheered on its team to the stirring words of "Long, Long Ago;" the class of '95 answered with "Hold the Fort."

There probably wasn't a dry eye in Northampton.

What followed after that was a misunderstanding that set the women's game back 75 years — The Clara Baer Story.

In 1895 Clara Baer was a physical education instructor at Newcomb College in New Orleans. She had heard of the wonders of basketball and had written Naismith for a copy of its rules.

The Doc sent her a diagram of the court and, ever helpful, penciled lines on the court to suggest where the various players might best be positioned.

Clara Baer misinterpreted this to mean that the players could not leave those areas. Thus was born the strange breed of basketball, at least for the women, in which players were restricted to specific areas of the floor.

Baer called this game, and will the strong feminists among you please close your eyes, "Basquette."

She subsequently said the modified rules of "Basquette" were necessary because "basketball as originally arranged needed to be adapted to the use of women and growing girls; a game where a delicate girl, unac-

59

customed to exercise, and for the most part adverse to it, would become interested in spite of herself.''

The additional bad news was that her rules, heartily endorsed by most male and female educators of the day, including James Naismith, soon became institutionalized nationwide.

''It has been found,'' read the introduction to the women's basketball rules book of the day, ''that a number of girls who play without division lines have developed hypertrophy of the heart.''

These women's rules, formally adopted by a four-woman committee in 1899, forbade one player to steal the ball from another, mandated that a woman could not hold the ball anyplace on the court for more than three seconds, and divided the court into three distinct sections. Any player who crossed a line was guilty of a personal foul. In fact, there was so much fear nationwide that women would be passing out like sun-struck turkeys at just the sight of a basketball, that many states even forbade women to play the game in high school. But the women's game would survive anyway. On April 4, 1895, a women's team from the University of California met a team from Stanford, which was apparently one of the first intercollegiate games.

The women's game also suffered from the same pattern of rule changes and interpretations that had plagued the men's game. The number of players allowed on a women's team changed over the years; until 1899 a women's team could have anywhere from five to ten players. That was later changed to anywhere from five to nine players, and after 1922 the spread was from six to nine players.

In 1937 the number was dropped to six, where it stayed for many years. But of the six, three had to be on offense and three on defense, which made for a weaker game. In some areas of the country it would be another 30 years before women played basketball with only five on a team. Nor was it until 1938 before the women's court was divided into two instead of three sections, and it took several more decades to get it down to one regulation court.

For a long time women were not allowed to dribble the basketball. In the 1950s only one dribble was allowed before a shot or pass, a number that was generously expanded to three dribbles in the 1960s. In today's equal-opportunity game, both sexes can and do dribble at will.

In Iowa, where girl's high school basketball is bigger than hog feed, the girls still play mostly six-on-a-side and the state finals are sold out every year.

Overall, the popularity of women's basketball couldn't hope to rival that of the men in its early days; there were too many social forces working against it. But in the early and mid 1900s it was still among the most popular of women's team games, probably for lack of competition.

It was helped along by the Edmonton Commercial Grads, a Canadian

THE SATURDAY EVENING POST

An Illustrated Weekly Magazine
Founded A. D. 1728 by Benj. Franklin

OCT. 6, 1906 5c. THE COPY

VASSAR: Delicious but Dyspeptic—By WALLACE IRWIN

THE CURTIS PUBLISHING COMPANY, PHILADELPHIA

Top left: Typical bloomer-type uniforms worn by women who first played basketball at the turn of the century. Top right: The popularity of basketball was evident 15 years after the game was invented and 13 years after the first women's game. A Vassar basketball player was featured on the cover of the Saturday Evening Post *October 6, 1906. Bottom: The quiet symmetry of a turn-of-the-century New England high school team.*

61

Taylors Trunk's team of Chicago.

1942, ballet of Basketball Golden Jubilee held in Memphis, Tenn.

women's team that overcame an amazingly dull name with amazingly good basketball. Between 1915 and 1940, the mighty Grads won 522 games and lost 20. They were world-wide barnstormers, traveling 125,000 miles across Canada, the United States and Europe.

The Grads won 14 Canadian championships and won 24 straight games in the European cities of Paris, Amsterdam and Berlin as an adjunct to Olympic festivities. They once captured 147 games in a row, and yes, whipped men's teams seven of the nine times they met.

Who were these women and what were they doing winning all those games?

Amazingly, almost all of them (and there were only 38 different women on the team in all those 25 years) graduated from the same commercial high school in Edmonton, Canada.

Hence the name Commercial Grads.

Their coach was the redoubtable John Percy Page, a man who preached a Grad must be "a lady first and a basketball player second" at a time when people really believed that.

His Grads were mostly teachers and stenographers. They had no gym, played home games outdoors, practiced endlessly on simple but very effective plays, and eventually developed a four-tiered farm system that led from the local high school team to the touring club. The rules were so restrictive that any Grad who married had to resign from the team.

Such touring clubs, some with company sponsorship and some that played Globetrotter-like exhibition games, offered one of the few outlets there were for women who wanted to keep playing basketball after high school or college.

Another outlet was the Amateur Athletic Union, which began a national tournament in Los Angeles in 1926. The immortal Mildred "Babe" Didrikson led her Employers Casualty Company "Golden Cyclones" to the AAU championship in 1931, scoring 106 points in five tournament games. The Babe was an AAU All-American three years, before she went off to the world of track and field and professional golf.

Other early legends of the game were Alline Banks Sprouse, an AAU All-American 11 straight years, and Corine Jaax Smith, honored nine times between 1931 and 1945.

In the 1970s the Association for Intercollegiate Athletics for Women — say that quick 10 times — began sponsoring national championships. Immaculata of Philadelphia won the national championship in 1972, '73, and '74 and Delta State of Cleveland, Mississippi, won the next three years.

The women's game finally crept into the Really Big Time in February, 1975, when Immaculata College of Philadelphia beat Queens College of New York 65-61 before 12,000 screaming fans in Madison Square Garden. This was an era when Montclair State's Carol Blazejowski, who averaged 31.7

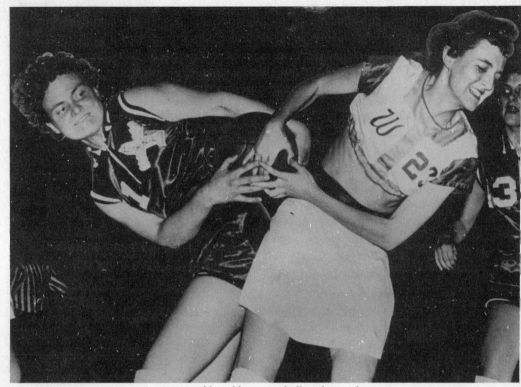

An age-old problem, one ball and two players.

points a game over three seasons, Old Dominion's Nancy Lieberman, UCLA's Ann Meyers, and Lynette Woodard of Kansas would finally establish the women's game.

Another big boost came from a Roman numeral, Title IX, a mandate from the federal government in 1978 that women's athletic programs be given equality with men's. Title IX has helped, but is still far short of its goal.

In 1982, after a bitter fight with the AIAW, the NCAA began sponsoring a national tournament in women's basketball. Louisiana Tech was the first winner, and players like Pam Kelly of Louisiana Tech, Anne Donovan of Old Dominion, Pam and Paula McGee of USC and, of course, Cheryl Miller of USC, led the game into the 20th century.

Women's basketball wasn't even allowed into the Olympics until 1976, some 40 years after Naismith had witnessed the men's teams playing in the 1936 Olympics in Berlin.

In 1984, the U.S. Olympic team, led by Miller, won the gold medal from the mighty Russians in Los Angeles.

There have been several attempts to form women's professional basketball leagues over the years, most of which ended in bankruptcy court instead of on a basketball court.

For the record, the first game of the Women's Professional Basketball League was played between the Chicago Hustle and the Milwaukee Does on December 9, 1978. The Hustle won 92-87 with Debra Waddy-Rossow scoring 30 points.

Ann Meyers, former Olympic and UCLA basketball star, became the first woman to sign with an NBA team. She signed a one-year-guaranteed $50,000 contract with the Indiana Pacers on August 30, 1979, but never made it into an NBA game.

Arkansas Gems (Clown Jewels of Basketball).

Chapter 8
WHERE HAVE YOU GONE, HANK LUISETTI?
The amazing early years of college basketball

Hiram College, winners of World's Intercollegiate Basket Ball Championship, St. Louis, 1904.

The college game as we know it, with its 50,000-seat domed stadiums, illegal recruiting, Las Vegas-style dance teams, NCAA tournament and $300,000-a-year coaches, is a slightly different game from what The Doc had in mind. In fact, we're all hard-pressed to remember the game was original-ly invented to entertain the Christians, not the lions. But the growth of the college game was inevitable. It spread as surely as Naismith's YMCA classmates and students spread across the country, and the world, to other YMCAs and universities.

By 1896, four years after the first known dribble, the nation's YMCAs already had a national championship tournament. But the college game evolved separately from the YMCA game and more slowly. The college lads stayed close to their own tiny gyms, if they bothered to use gyms at all. Naismith, you see, had envisioned his game being played indoors or out, with the number of collegians on a team determined by the size of the court, or cow pasture.

His original guidelines said if the playing surface was less than 1,800 square feet, five men could play on a side. If the surface was 1,800 to 3,600 square feet, seven could play on a side. Anything larger required nine to a side.

To help you get a feel for this, today's college court is 94 feet by 50 feet, or 4,700 square feet — easily qualifying for nine men on a side.

Welcome to the 3-4-2 zone defense.

In 1893, Amos Alonzo Stagg left Springfield and took basketball to the University of Chicago. In January, 1896, a Chicago team played the University of Iowa in an interstate tilt, but the Iowa team was actually a YMCA team composed of Iowa students. Chicago won 15-12; neither team substituted. The Minnesota State School of Mines had dug past Hamline College on February 9, 1895, but that game doesn't quite count either, because each team had nine on a side.

Thus history would have it that the first, true, collegiate men's game was played between Yale and Penn in 1897. Yale's Bulldogs dogged 'em, 32-10.

Yale, Harvard, Princeton, Columbia and Cornell formed a basketball league in 1901 and Yale won it with a 6-2 record. Another league composed of Amherst, Holy Cross, Williams, Dartmouth and Trinity started about the same time.

Those are schools rarely seen in today's Top 20 basketball polls. But, as in collegiate football, the eastern Ivy League schools formed the cradle that rocked the sport.

It was about this time that a few of the nation's YMCAs, seeing the gym-nasiums dominated by rough and tumble basketball games, actually began to ban the games — the son had already begun to break away from the father.

By 1904 college basketball had grown to the point where exhibition games

January 27, 1937 — An early action photo of a game between Springfield College and St. Francis College.

were played at the Olympic games held in conjunction with the St. Louis World Fair.

An outdoor court was set up inside the Olympic stadium, and mighty Hiram College captured what was then called the Olympic World's Intercollegiate Basket Ball Championship.

"Gimmie an H . . ."

"Gimmie an I . . ."

Bring on UCLA.

OK, the game still had some growing up to do. Back then few college teams had, or even wanted, coaches. Those pioneer teams played a mishmash schedule of college, YMCA, Amateur Athletic Union and even professional teams. There wasn't even ESPN.

Basketball was still a regional game with about four regional flavors: some teams ran, some stalled, some dribbled, and some didn't — or didn't know how.

A few areas even stuck with the concept of dividing the floor into sections, with each player a specialist and very little all-around play.

Incredibly enough, until 1914 colleges were still using the original Naismith rule that said, ". . . when a ball goes out-of-bounds, it shall be thrown back into the field by the first player touching it."

Think about that for a few seconds. The team that first touched a ball AFTER it had gone out of bounds retained possession. If an errant pass or shot went down a stairwell or into the balcony, players from both teams could go thundering after it, trampling all spectators and popcorn salesmen in their path.

It was to prevent this mayhem that entire basketball courts were enclosed in wire mesh, chicken wire or even metal cages.

The man given credit for first wrapping a court with chicken wire was one Fred Padderatz, who actually managed a Trenton, N. J., professional team. He had watched the ball go sailing off one too many times, so he wrapped the court in chicken wire eight feet high.

The concept was very popular for a time. Some teams, in fact, used rope netting draped 10 to 15 feet high around the court, thus keeping the combatants bouncing around inside like professional wrestlers.

And that is how basketball players became known as cagers.

College basketball moved west in the very early 1900s with the formation of the Western Intercollegiate Basket Ball League, which included the University of Chicago, Illinois, Purdue, Minnesota, and Wisconsin. In another five years, far western schools such as California, Oregon and Washington were forming associations that moved basketball coast to coast.

In 1905 long-distance road games were invented, with Wisconsin and Minnesota both traveling east to play Columbia, which was then, believe it or not, the first "Beast from the East."

Columbia won both games and probably would have been declared national champion had anyone cared enough to name one. But the NIT and NCAA tourneys were still decades away, and the Associated Press didn't begin Top 20 national rankings until 1949.

So college basketball became popular almost in spite of itself. Many teams played what was called the "standing zone defense," a picturesque and exciting ploy where everybody just stood there clogging up the middle.

Here were big schools like Iowa, Minnesota, Washington and Oregon, that had already built field houses holding 10,000 people, and college ball was bogged down with a jump ball after every basket, excessive stalling and rough play that bordered on barbarous.

OK, there was *some* progress. In 1921, the two words in the game's title were officially merged into one — basketball.

Basketball historians like to point to Ned Irish, a New York sportswriter who promoted college basketball doubleheaders in old Madison Square

Garden, as the man most responsible for the 1930s boom in basketball, and it's hard to argue with that notion.

New York was already a basketball hothouse. So when Irish began pitting the best of The City against teams from well south and west of the Hudson River, he was soon drawing 16,000 a game in a town where 2,500 had been the norm.

Teams such as Long Island University, City College of New York and New York University were then as strong as any teams in the country. So when Irish matched them up against a Kentucky or a Stanford (then a national powerhouse), he was guaranteed a sellout.

Then there was Angelo "Hank" Luisetti.

Luisetti, from Stanford, came along at a time when most people were still shooting set shots with two hands, and free throws underhanded.

Two hands were the norm. That was the style God and Naismith had in mind. So here came this handsome, personable, dark-haired guy out of California tossing the ball up there one-handed. Some of them were even close to a jump shot.

This was like watching the sun come up in the west. Yet on the night of December 30, 1936, when Luisetti scored 15 points as Stanford beat Long Island University to break its three-year winning streak, a lot of people began thinking and shooting one-handed.

Luisetti hadn't invented the one-handed shot, but he did give it credence, much to the dismay of conservative, old-line coaches everywhere.

Years later a Holy Cross star named Bob Cousy would give coaches similar fits by dribbling the ball behind his back, a move most experts said had no place in basketball.

Those coaches ordered their charges never to dribble like Bob Cousy. The kids said, "yes sir," and then went off into a distant corner and practiced dribbling behind their backs.

Now any kid old enough to spell Air Jordan can dribble behind his back. Their coaches, in fact, insist on it.

So with people like Hank Luisetti, college basketball staggered forward in the 1930s. By 1940 a few games were televised on a regional basis, and closed-circuit television was fairly common.

The game took another great leap forward in the mid-1940s when Kenny Sailors of Wyoming brought his fully-developed, one-handed jump shot to Madison Square Garden and helped his team win the NCAA.

A few of the western schools had moved far ahead of the east in shooting styles, but, as always, the show had to be taken to New York to give it national exposure.

In the giddy New York environment of the 1930s a national playoff seemed inevitable. In 1938 the Metropolitan Basketball Writers Association inaugurated the National Invitational Tournament by inviting six of the best teams in the country to Madison Square Garden to compete for a national championship.

The six teams invited to the first NIT were New York University, Long Island University, Bradley, Temple, Colorado and Oklahoma A & M.

Temple beat Colorado, led by now-Supreme Court Justice Byron "Whizzer" White, 60 to 36 to claim the first national title.

A year later the NCAA got into the national championship picture with its own tournament by selecting eight teams from different regions of the country.

The first NCAA championship game matched the East regional winner, Ohio State, against the West regional winner, Oregon, in a game played at Northwestern. Oregon won 46-33.

The NCAA tournament was not satisfactory, however, because only one

This original painting in the Naismith Basketball Hall of Fame depicts Hank Luisetti of Stanford shooting his one-handed shot that revolutionized the game of basketball.

team could be selected from a region, although it might have two or three teams worthy of claiming a national title. In those early years, in fact, a team could play in both the NIT and the NCAA tourneys — and the NIT was considered the better and more prestigious tourney, as would remain the case until the 1950s.

Soon the NIT and the NCAA were locked in a power struggle for the better teams, with the NCAA, as the governing force in college basketball, practically forcing its member schools into its tournament.

The eight-team NCAA format grew to 16 teams in 1951, and then to 22 in 1953. From 1952 to 1974, the number of teams invited to the tournament fluctuated between 22 and 25. In 1974 the tournament went to 32 teams, then 40 in 1979, 48 in 1980, 52 in 1983 and 53 in 1984. Finally it evolved into the 64-team, television-dominated, office-pool-generating, multi-million-dollar monster we all know and love. From 1985 until 1990 there will be 64 teams in the NCAA tournament, with some coaches advocating it should be open to all of the more than 200 NCAA Division I schools.

The NIT, now a tournament for 32 of "the rest of the teams," still endures, but only its Final Four games are held in New York.

The forerunner of highly-ranked teams in the 1940s and 1950s — the undefeated 1912 University of Kentucky Wildcats.

LEADING COLLEGE TEAMS BY
DECADE (1900 - 1959)

The following chart shows the top teams in won-lost percentage during each decade. It is interesting to note the major turnover from one decade to the next and that most of the basketball powers of recent years are not listed.

1900-1909

	WON	LOST	PCT.
Chicago	78	12	.867
Dayton	61	10	.859
Oregon State	62	15	.805
Minnesota	107	29	.787
Michigan St.	76	22	.776
Montana St.	39	12	.765
CCNY	25	10	.714
Wisconsin	75	30	.714

1910-1919

	WON	LOST	PCT.
Navy	109	9	.924
Creighton	63	6	.913
California	52	11	.825
Texas	102	26	.813
Wisconsin	129	34	.791
Virginia	101	27	.789
VPI	118	36	.766
Penn State	94	33	.740
Kansas State	94	37	.718
Syracuse	98	39	.715

1920-1929

	WON	LOST	PCT.
Montana St.	213	44	.829
Army	135	34	.811
Navy	145	37	.797
CCNY	108	30	.782
Notre Dame	170	49	.776
California	125	39	.768
N. Carolina	158	48	.767
Creighton	142	44	.764
Oklahoma	93	29	.762
Penn State	113	38	.748

1930-1939

	WON	LOST	PCT.
Long Island	201	38	.841
Kentucky	161	34	.826
St. John's	184	41	.818
Kansas	153	37	.805
Syracuse	143	37	.794
Purdue	148	39	.791
Western Ky.	197	52	.791
CCNY	119	35	.773
Washington	195	62	.759
DePaul	142	45	.759

1940-1949

	WON	LOST	PCT.
Kentucky	240	41	.854
Seton Hall	128	23	.848
Hamline	199	41	.829
Okla. State	237	55	.812
Rhode Is.	179	43	.806
Eastern Ky.	126	32	.797
Duquesne	118	32	.787
Long Island	179	49	.785
Western Ky.	222	66	.771
Tennessee	150	49	.754

1950-1959

	WON	LOST	PCT.
Kentucky	224	33	.872
N. C. State	242	65	.788
Seattle	232	68	.773
Dayton	228	71	.763
LaSalle	209	65	.763
Holy Cross	198	65	.753
Kansas State	179	63	.740
Hamline	195	70	.736
Connecticut	187	67	.736
W. Virginia	205	74	.735

The amazing college teams of the early years included:

CHICAGO, 1907-09

There may have been better collegiate teams in pre-"modern era" years, but no other team dominated the national scene as did the University of Chicago squad of 1907-08-09.

The top man of those teams was John Schommer, who led the Big Ten in scoring for three straight years as Chicago won the title each time (sharing it with co-champion Wisconsin in 1907). His lifetime conference average was just over 10 points a game. He made the Helms All-America each year and was selected player of the year in 1909.

KANSAS, 1922-23

Forrest (Phog) Allen first coached Kansas to national championships in 1922 and 1923 and won another one in 1952. In his career, he coached college basketball for 40 years, 39 at Kansas, and had an all-time record of 771 wins against 233 losses. Allen won 24 conference championships at Kansas and also coached at Warrensburg Teachers, Baker and Haskell Institute.

His 1922 team won 16 and lost 2, and in 1923 had a 17-1 mark. In winning its second consecutive national title, Kansas held opponents to a mere 16.6 points per game. The Jayhawks' two great guards, Paul Endacott and Charles Black, were honored for their fine defensive play with berths on the 1923 Helms All-American squad. Endacott also made the honor team the year before.

PITTSBURGH, 1928, 1930

Pitt dominated the national collegiate scene in 1928, going undefeated in 21 games and repeated the #1 rating in 1930 on the basis of a 23-2 mark. Guard Sykes Reed and forward Chuck Hyatt were the team leaders in 1928 and Hyatt was still going strong with the 1930 team. H. Clifford Carlson was the team's coach.

PURDUE, 1930, 1932

Led by John Wooden, All-American in 1930, 1931 and 1932, Purdue won the 1930 and 1932 Big Ten titles and won the mythical national title the latter year. In 1930 the Boilermakers were undefeated in 10 conference games and in '32 they won 11 of 12. In their national championship year, they averaged nearly 40 points a game, while limiting opponents to about 25.

Ward (Piggy) Lambert coached the team in 1917 and from 1919 to 1949. He developed many fine teams, but the 1932 squad was rated his best.

74

MONTANA STATE, 1929

The Montana State "Wonder Team" of 1929 won 35 of 37 games. This was one of the most extensive schedules played by a college team up to that time. Coach Schubert R. Dyche's team averaged slightly over 60 points a game, an amazing average for that time, and held opponents to an average of about 32. The team scored over 100 points once and went over 90 four other times, which would be impressive even now.

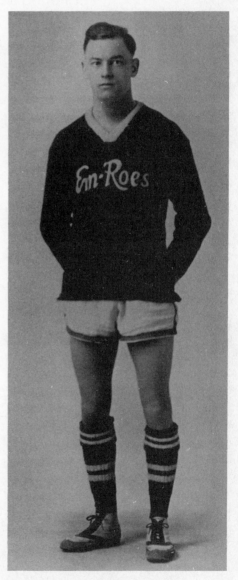

Top left: Dr. "Phog" Allen succeeded Dr. Naismith as Kansas University coach, 1907-08. Right: Ward "Piggy" Lambert, 1914. Bottom left: Paul Endacott.

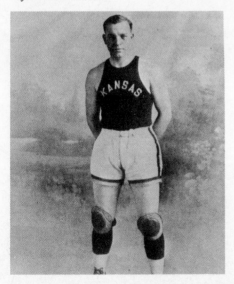

Chapter 9
MARCH MADNESS
TAKES OVER
The amazing expanding
college tournaments

The Astrodome in Houston, January 28, 1968, as Houston rallies past UCLA 71-69.
This game set a college attendance record (52,693) which stood for over 14 years.

In the past 50 years college basketball has expanded to include men and women playing in the NCAA (Division I, II, and III), the NAIA, the "college" division and junior college division, just to name a half-dozen.

Here are a few amazing facts about that growth.

• The eight teams in the first NCAA tournament were selected from each of eight geographic districts, by committees. The system was so strange that only one team was chosen from a district that included Alabama, Florida, Georgia, Kentucky, Louisiana, Maryland, Mississippi, North Carolina, South Carolina, Tennessee and Virginia. Another district included Arizona, Arkansas and Texas. That first tournament, held in Evanston, Illinois, in 1939 *lost* $2,531.

• In what added a nice, if not poetic, touch to the affair, Indiana played Springfield College, The Doc's old school, on the way to the 1940 NCAA championship. Indiana routed Springfield College 48-24, and then defeated Kansas 60-42 for the title. The tournament made a profit of $9,590 and each winning team received $750.

• Western schools dominated the NCAA tournament in its first eight years, with Oregon, Stanford, Wyoming, Utah and Oklahoma A&M (a double winner) taking six titles. In 1943 Wyoming, with Kenny Sailors putting up the first effective jump shots in basketball history, beat Georgetown 46-34 for the title. It took Georgetown almost 40 years to recover.

• In 1943 a post-season game matching NCAA champ Wyoming and NIT winner St. John's was held as a World War II Red Cross benefit. Wyoming won 52-47, but the victory did nothing to calm the NIT-NCAA war.

• The war continued in 1944 when Utah turned down an NCAA bid because the association would not guarantee travel expenses. The NIT did agree to pay Utah's expenses to New York, but the Utes were beaten in the first round by Kentucky. Utah went home, only to receive a second call from the NCAA; Arkansas, which had accepted the NCAA bid in Utah's place, had two players hurt in a car accident and could not compete. Utah accepted the second chance, went to the NCAA tournament and outlasted Dartmouth 42-40 in the championship game.

If that wasn't enough, Utah then played St. John's, the NIT winner, in a second Red Cross benefit game. The Utes won 43-36, the second year in a row the NCAA champ had beaten the NIT champion.

• In 1949 Kentucky accepted bids from both the NCAA and the NIT, which was legal at the time, and had visions of winning both. The cocky Wildcats lost in the first round of the NIT to Loyola of Chicago in Madison Square Garden. Adolph Rupp then took his team 3,000 miles by train to the NCAA championships in Seattle, Washington, where the Wildcats whipped Oklahoma A&M 46-36 for the title.

- In 1950 City College of New York became the only team to win the NIT and the NCAA tournament the same year. On March 19, 1950, CCNY surprised Bradley 69-61 in Madison Square Garden to win the NIT. Ten days later CCNY defeated (who else?) Bradley 71-68 in (where else?) Madison Square Garden to win the NCAA and complete this unique accomplishment. A year later almost all that CCNY team confessed to accepting bribes from gamblers to "fix" games during the 1949-50 season.
- In 1951 the NCAA expanded its tournament to 16 teams, selecting teams with the best won-lost percentages in 10 major conferences, plus six at-large teams. Kentucky beat Kansas State in the final game 68-58, winning its third NCAA title in four years.
- By 1955 basketball power had moved east, with Kansas in 1952 the only team west of the Mississippi to win in the previous eight years. Big Bill Russell and his San Francisco Dons changed that, capturing titles in 1955 and 1956, while winning 56 games in a row.
- In 1962 for the first (and only) time in history, the same teams as the year before met in the NCAA title game. In 1961 the Number 2 Cincinnati Bearcats had beaten top-ranked Ohio State in overtime, 70-65. The losing Buckeyes included Jerry Lucas, John Havlicek and reserve Bobby Knight. The next year Cincinnati had considerably less trouble, earning a 71-59 victory. They were led by center Paul Hogue's 22 points and 19 rebounds.
- In 1963 Loyola of Chicago staged an incredible comeback to end the Bearcats' hopes of becoming the first college team to win three straight NCAA championships. Cincinnati was 15 points ahead with 12 minutes left. However, a possession game backfired and Loyola won in overtime, 60-58, on Vic Rouse's rebound basket just ahead of the buzzer.
- Between 1964, when the Bruins beat Duke 98-83 for the championship, and 1975, when Kentucky fell 92-85, UCLA dominated college basketball like the town bully at an ice-cream social.

Only Texas Western in 1966 (which also beat Kentucky) and North Carolina State in 1974 (beating Marquette) interrupted the Bruins' charge. UCLA won 10 championships in 12 years, including seven in a row. Even in 1974 when North Carolina State took the title, UCLA finished third.

The Maestro of this reign was John Wooden, the Wizard of Westwood, who hung up his coach's whistle in 1975 with a career 667-161 record.

- In the first 12 years after UCLA's domination ended, Indiana won three titles, Louisville two, and the other titles were split among seven other schools.
- In the spring of 1987, CBS signed a three-year contract for the rights to the tournament that will pay the NCAA $166.2 million, about $68 million more than the old contract.

The NCAA championship game in Madison Square Garden, March 25, 1947. Holy Cross won over Oklahoma 58-47.

The 30 conferences with automatic qualifiers to the men's tournament will receive $90,000 a year and the 18 automatic conference qualifiers in the women's tournament will get about $30,000 each. The NCAA said each Final Four team in the 1987 tournament received $1,056,027 and the 32 first-round losers received a minimum of $211,205.

Current official NCAA basketballs.

AMAZING LIST OF THE ALL-TIME NCAA CHAMPIONSHIP TOURNAMENT SCORERS

Player	Games	Points	Average
Elvin Hayes	13	358	27.5
Oscar Robertson	10	324	32.4
Lew Alcindor	12	304	25.3
Bill Bradley	9	303	33.7
Austin Carr	7	289	41.3
Jerry West	9	275	30.6
Jerry Lucas	12	266	22.2
Bill Walton	12	254	21.2

There is no better proof of basketball cream coming to the top than this collection of stars.

Jerry West and Jerry Lucas.

Oscar Robertson as a high school star.

AMAZING MVP QUIZ

Match these most valuable players from early NCAA tournaments with their respective teams.

Team	Player
1. Indiana	A. Howard Dallmar
2. Oklahoma State	B. Irwin Dambrot
3. Wisconsin	C. Arnie Ferrin
4. Wyoming	D. Alex Groza
5. Holy Cross	E. Marvin Huffman
6. Kentucky	F. George Kaftan
7. CCNY	G. John Kotz
8. Utah	H. Bob Kurland
9. Stanford	I. Clyde Lovellette
10. Kansas	J. Ken Sailors

AMAZING NIT QUIZ

The National Invitational Tournament was started in 1938 by the Metropolitan Basketball Writers Association. It proved so embarrassingly successful that the writers quickly turned it over to the folks at Madison Square Garden to operate. See if you can answer the following questions about the NIT.

1. One of the Colorado players in the first NIT championship, won by Temple 60-36, would later become a U. S. Supreme Court justice. He was   (A) Judge Roy Bean   (B) Earl Warren   (C) "Whizzer" White   (D) "Leak" Mason   (E) Louis Brandeis.

2. DePaul won the 1945 NIT with a dominating center who revolutionized the college game and helped establish professional basketball. The big center was   (A) Bob Kurland   (B) Bevo Francis   (C) Nate Thurmond   (D) George Mikan   (E) Jim Ringo.

3. St. Louis University won the 1948 NIT championship over New York University, 65-52. The St. Louis squad's nickname, the Billikens, was bad enough, but still didn't compare with NYU, which was nicknamed (A) the Big Green Machine   (B) the Fighting Violets   (C) the Yellow Roses of Long Island   (D) the Little Blue Men   (E) the Fighting Crimson.

81

4. In 1954 La Salle defeated Bradley 92-76 to win the NIT title, but partly because of the 1950s basketball scandals, that NIT game was not played in New York. It was played in   (A) Philadelphia   (B) Kansas City   (C) Boston   (D) Louisville   (E) Bangor, Maine.

5. Southern Illinois, led by a sensational guard, won the NIT title in 1967, beating Marquette 71-56. That guard was   (A) "Smokin' Joe" Frazier   (B) Freddie Brown   (C) Bill Bradley   (D) Walt Frazier   (E) Bo Lamar.

6. The 1987 NIT was won by   (A) La Salle   (B) Wake Forest   (C) Southern Mississippi   (D) Pittsburgh   (E) Bellarmine.

Kentucky captures the 1958 NCAA championship in Freedom Hall, Louisville, by conquering Seattle and Elgin Baylor, 84-72.

Here are a few amazing NCAA statistics to close the chapter.

• Doug Grayson of Kent State hit 16 consecutive field goals against North Carolina on December 6, 1967, still the NCAA record. He hit 18 of 19 shots for the game.

• Ray Voelkel of American University hit 25 consecutive shots in 1978, but it took Voelkel, apparently a very cautious fella, nine games to do it. It's a wonder anyone noticed.

• Jay Handlan of Washington and Lee took 71 shots against Furman on February 17, 1951, hitting 30, a 42 percent figure that probably irritated 100 percent of his teammates.

• Danny Ainge, an expert in irritation, set an NCAA mark by scoring in double figures in 112 consecutive games at Brigham Young.

• Pete Maravich put up 3,166 field goal attempts in his career at LSU and scored 3,667 points.

• UCLA's Bill Walton hit 21 of 22 shots against Memphis State in the NCAA championship game in 1973 and looked like he could have done it barefoot.

• Notre Dame's Austin Carr scored 61 points in an NCAA game against Ohio (the university not the state) on March 3, 1970.

• Purdue's Rick Mount took 36 shots against Louisville in 1969 and missed 24 of them. Ray Voelkel probably never missed 24 shots in his college career.

• David Robinson of Navy blocked 14 shots in a 1986 game against North Carolina-Wilmington.

• Nevada-Las Vegas scored 164 points, the NCAA record, against Hawaii-Hilo in 1976 while holding the islanders to 111.

• Kentucky and Mississippi combined for 108 rebounds in a game on February 8, 1964, which means, of course, the teams missed at least 108 shots. Where have you gone, Ray Voelkel?

AMAZING NIT QUIZ ANSWERS

1. (C) "Whizzer" White
2. (D) George Mikan
3. (B) the Fighting Violets
4. (B) Kansas City
5. (D) Walt Frazier
6. (C) Southern Mississippi

AMAZING MVP QUIZ ANSWERS

1. E   6. D
2. H   7. B
3. G   8. C
4. J   9. A
5. F   10. I

Chapter 10
SOMETHING'S ROTTEN IN THE GARDEN
Amazing scandals

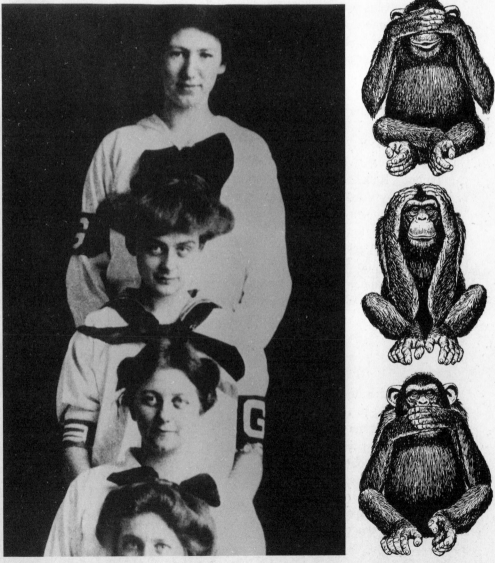

The innocence of basketball's early days disappeared. The first rule of college basketball in the late 1940s became "see no evil, hear no evil, speak no evil."

Many of the people who watched college basketball grow — the sports-writers, the coaches and maybe a few of the fans — had a feeling in the late 1940s that something was sour in their game.

Sportswriters wondered about games that were closer than they should have been, and murmured dark rumors about bookies and gamblers. Some coaches, beginning a refrain that has never died, complained about illegal recruiting, alumni payoffs to players, and the pressure to win above all else. A few fans worried about those problems, but others were too busy betting on the games.

An early sign that things were going wrong appeared in 1944. Vadal Peterson, coach of the University of Utah, said he knocked down a gambler who was bold enough to come to his hotel room and ask how much it would cost to have Utah lose to Dartmouth in the 1944 NCAA finals.

According to a story in *The New York Times,* one gambler had actually run out onto the floor and kissed a Utah player who made a last-second goal against Kentucky in the 1943 NIT. The basket had cut Kentucky's winning margin to eight points and the betting line was ten points; that one basket saved the gambler $15,000.

"Betting on college games is going to create a scandal 'that will stink to high heaven' unless college presidents intercede to save the game," warned Kansas Coach Phog Allen in October, 1944. "There hasn't been enough publicity given known cases where bribes were taken."

The smell began to leak out of the college game in earnest in January, 1945. Then New York police, staking out the home of a suspected fence, instead confronted two players from Brooklyn College. The players panicked and admitted to police that they and three of their teammates had split $1,000 to dump the Brooklyn College-Akron game.

The sports world sat up, but didn't listen too carefully. The five players were expelled from school. The two gamblers were fined $500 each and sentenced to a year in prison.

"Your bribery of these young men was a dastardly act of the vilest kind made in order to permit you and your cheating, chiseling, crooked henchmen to reap benefits of bets made with an unsuspected and innocent public," said Judge Louis Goldstein at the May, 1945, hearing. "Nothing concerned you except to fill your pockets with crooked money."

There was one footnote to the case. After the five players were expelled, it was learned that one of them, Larry Pearlstein, had never enrolled as a student.

In September, 1945, an attempt was made to bribe a student at George Washington University. The player, David Shapiro, went along with the gamblers while reporting the incident to the New York County District Attorney, Frank S. Hogan. In February, 1946, four gamblers were found guilty of offering Shapiro from $500 to $1,000 a game and were sentenced to prison for from one to two and one-half years.

Still, the stench was getting stronger. In January, 1951, two Manhattan College players confessed to fixing three games in the 1949-50 season for $1,000 a game. The players, Henry E. Poppe and John A. Byrnes, were co-captains of the team. The only bright spot was that Poppe and Byrnes were caught after Poppe and a few gamblers tried to convince Junius Kellogg, another Manhattan player, to throw a game for $1,000. Instead, Kellogg told his coach and helped trap the others.

But the college gambling story didn't stop there. In February, 1951, three members of the City College of New York team that had won both the NIT and the NCAA the year before admitted taking $1,500 each for shaving points in games during that current season. Just ten days later those three players, Ed Roman, Ed Warner and Al Roth, were joined by a fourth, Floyd Lane, who admitted to "point fixing."

Two days later three Long Island University basketball players, team captain Adolph Bigos, LeRoy Smith and Sherman White, who had led the nation in scoring, admitted taking $1,850 to fix four games that season and three the year before.

After that, the collegiate dam burst. In July, 1951, eight Bradley University players admitted taking $6,700 in bribes to hold down the score in two games. The players included All-American guard Gene Melchiorre, team captain William Mann, Charles Grover, Aaron Preece and James Kelly. As a result, the NCAA refused to let Bradley play in the 1953 NCAA tournament.

Two days later the University of Toledo was implicated in point-shaving, but no names were listed.

In October, 1951, three former University of Kentucky stars, Ralph Beard, Alex Groza and Dale Barnstable, admitted they had been given $1,500 to "shave" points in the March 14, 1949, NIT first round game against Loyola, a game that favored Kentucky lost 67-56. The Wildcats went on after that game to win the NCAA championship.

In August, 1952, the Southeastern Conference suspended Kentucky from basketball competition. In November, 1952, an NCAA council put Kentucky on probation for a year for paying athletes and allowing ineligible players to play. The NCAA also recommended that other NCAA schools should refuse to play Kentucky that year. As a result, the school cancelled its entire 1952-53 season.

When the odor finally cleared and the New York grand jury that had pressed the investigation was dismissed, 32 players from seven schools were implicated in fixing 87 games during the 1948-51 seasons.

Before the investigation New York had been the undisputed center of college basketball. It hosted the NIT each year and had been host to the NCAA finals seven times between 1943 and 1950. There has not been an NCAA final held in New York since; even the NIT left town for a while after the scandals.

Melchiorre, the Bradley star, would later say of the scandals: "None of us had any money . . . We justified it by saying the colleges were making plenty of it . . . and it wasn't wrong because we weren't going to throw games."

College basketball did clean up its act a little after that, but there was still some dirt left under the rug. In 1961 two bookies were arrested for bribing players at Seton Hall University and the University of Connecticut. That scandal eventually spread to include several other schools in the Midwest and East Coast, but didn't have the impact of the earlier scandal.

The potential for college basketball scandals has not fully ended. In March, 1985, Tulane basketball star John "Hot Rod" Williams was indicted on five counts of conspiracy and bribery for allegedly shaving points in games against Memphis State and Southern Mississippi. Six Tulane students — three former teammates and three fraternity brothers — admitted being part of the conspiracy, and testified against Williams.

In August, 1985, the first trial against Williams ended in a mistrial. The second trial lasted six days and Williams was acquitted of all charges. Tulane, however, admitted its guilt to many NCAA violations occurring within the program and abandoned its basketball program. Williams went on to play professional basketball for the Cleveland Cavaliers.

Not all the basketball scandals were confined to the hardcourt. These East Coast college students were changed with aggravated basketball rustling, creating a nuisance outside a state capitol building and imitating Abe Lemons without a license. All charges were later dropped.

A former East Coast dog lover and plumber's assistant is shown here tearing up a locker room telephone number, following a particularly tough loss.

University of Kentucky coach Adolph Rupp and assistant coach Harry Lancaster read about the scandal involving their players.

MORE AMAZING ROTTEN STUFF IN BASKETBALL

★ A 1964 survey by the National Association of Basketball Coaches indicated that 12.8 percent of America's 330 major colleges were making illegal offers to high school recruits. About 40 percent of the recruits said illegal offers had been made to them. Of the schools willing to cheat, all had offered money, 80 percent offered cars, and more than half offered clothing. The survey said school alumni caused most of the problems.

★ The players are not the only people able to "control" basketball games. In 1957 John Fraser, a Missouri Valley Conference referee, was the whistle blower in nine consecutive games in which large amounts of money were bet on one side. In each game there were serious fluctuations in the point spread. The "smart money" won in eight of the nine games. Fraser was relieved of his duty in mid-season due to a "neck injury" and quietly resigned.

★ In 1986 Northeast Louisiana became the first school in NCAA history to have its women's basketball team placed on probation for recruiting violations. It was proof that equality had arrived in the women's game.

★ Not all rotten stuff has to be serious. A 1956 game between Wichita and Detroit at Wichita came to an unusual end. A Detroit player, his team down by a point, took a long shot with seconds remaining. Meanwhile, a Wichita fan had tossed his overcoat over the basket. The ball hit the coat as the game ended. The referees ran to their locker room, locked the door, and declared Detroit the winner.

Chapter 11
CHUCK COOPER CROSSES THE LINE
The amazing story of blacks in basketball

The Daytona Beach girls' team, 1915.

Any sports fan worth his weight in trivia knows that Jackie Robinson was the first black in the modern era of major league baseball.

Yet few sports fans know that Duquesne All-American Chuck Cooper was the first black drafted into the National Basketball Association, a league blacks have since come to dominate.

When the Boston Celtics drafted Cooper in the second round of the 1950 NBA draft, there were plenty of raised eyebrows, but not much was said.

Professional basketball — however racist — just wasn't important enough at that time to etch Cooper's name forever into the national sports consciousness as baseball did Robinson's.

Surely Cooper endured the racial curses and slurs that followed Robinson around America's cities, yet his name has been all but forgotten.

"But Walter," were the supposed words of a fellow NBA owner to Boston owner Walter Brown as Chuck Cooper was drafted, "don't you know he's a colored boy?"

"I don't give a damn if he's plaid," was Brown's supposed answer. "All I know is this kid can play basketball and I want him on the Boston Celtics."

Thus snapped the NBA color line, a line that was actually a yellow streak down the back of the NBA team owners who had long feared what having blacks in the NBA would do to attendance, and to team morale.

Black basketball players had long suffered with that line. In its early days the game spread to the black athletic clubs, high schools and colleges, but social pressures kept it there.

Even the integrated high schools often had arbitrary quotas; no more than one or two blacks were allowed per team, even if there were ten who deserved to play.

The few major colleges that would play blacks in the early years (and in some southern conferences it took until 1970) often had to make separate travel accommodations because many hotels and restaurants would not serve them.

Some southern teams would not even play in post-season tournaments if it meant they had to face teams with large numbers of blacks. College coaches found it easier — and often the alumni were happier — if blacks were kept out of the program.

The unspoken, if not closet racist, attitude of many coaches, who feared the pressure of playing blacks while needing their abilities on the court, was "Play one black at home, two on the road, and three when you're behind."

There were a few teams in black athletic clubs in New York, Brooklyn and Jersey City as early as 1906. Colleges such as Howard University, Lincoln University, Union University and Hampton Institute had teams by 1910.

Robert Douglas, coach of the Rens.

Jackie Robinson

Chuck Cooper 1950-51
stats for the Boston
Celtics:

Games	66
Assists	174
Rebounds	562
Fouls	219
Points	615
Scoring Average	9.3

Chuck Cooper

A Colored Intercollegiate Athletic Association was formed among smaller colleges. Men such as Wilbur Woods of Nebraska, Paul Robeson at Rutgers, George Gregory at Columbia and Sidat Singh at Syracuse were pioneers in the 1920s, '30s and '40s. The first black to be named to an All-American team was UCLA center Don Barksdale, who was honored in 1947.

Still, the only place a black man could continue playing basketball after college, at least before Chuck Cooper signed with the Boston Celtics, was with the fabled New York Rens or, later on, the Harlem Globetrotters.

The New York Rens, named after the Renaissance Casino in Harlem where they played their home games, barnstormed the country for 16 years, winning at least 100 games in each of their last 14 years, many against white professional teams. The mighty Rens would sometimes draw 12,000 people to their games, especially against the stronger white teams. In 1939, near the end of their reign, the Rens went 112-7.

They were the spirtual godfathers, if not rivals, of the fabulous Harlem Globetrotters, a team that is still cranking out humor and basketball good-will after 60 years on the road.

The Globetrotters were born in 1926 as part of the entertainment package in Chicago's Savoy Ballroom, a fairly common occurrence in an era when basketball had all the respectability of a bootlegger in church.

Called the Savoy Big Five, the team played two games a week in the ballroom, only to be replaced by a higher form of entertainment — roller skating.

Undismayed, team owner Abe Saperstein changed the name of his team to the Harlem Globetrotters and hit the road, opening his six-decade tour on January 27, 1927, in beautiful Hinckley, Illinois.

Playing a much straighter brand of basketball than would come to be their trademark, the Globetrotters, with a few team members who hadn't previously traveled 100 yards east of Chicago, finished the first season 101-7.

The Globetrotters were hardly an overnight success. Those large men often had to sleep in their Model-T Fords because hotels would not take them. Goose Tatum, Meadowlark Lemon and Marques Haynes were still years away.

In 1940 the Globetrotters won what was called The World Championship of Professional Basketball, beating George Halas' Chicago Bruins 31-29. They'd earlier defeated the defending champs, the Rens, 37-36. It actually took them until April, 1946, to book a game played overseas, and that in Hawaii.

In 1948, showing what they could do without the clowning, the Globetrotters stunned George Mikan and his Minneapolis Lakers 61-59 before a record Chicago Stadium crowd of 20,000.

Over the next 11 years the Trotters easily whipped traveling teams of the best college all-stars. In 1951 some 75,000 people, still the all-time record basketball crowd, watched them win a game in Berlin.

By then the NBA had begun to compete with Saperstein for black talent, although not always successfully. Who could forget the sight of 7-foot 2-inch Wilt Chamberlain, who'd dropped out of Kansas early, playing point guard for the Globetrotters before he began his NBA career?

The door to the NBA began to open for blacks with the drafting of Cooper in 1950, the same year the Washington Capitols drafted the second black, Earl Lloyd of West Virginia State, in the eighth round. And that June, two months after the draft, the New York Knicks purchased Sweetwater Clifton from the Globetrotters and put him to work in New York.

There is no doubt Chuck Cooper was the first black drafted into the NBA, but the question as to the first black player to ever appear in an NBA game is still the source of mild debate. It could have been any of the three.

The NBA schedule for 1950 shows that Washington, which drafted Lloyd, opened the season that year on October 31. Boston didn't open until November 1, so it's very possible Lloyd was the first black to get into a game. But Lloyd

1938-39 New York Renaissance team, left to right: Willie Smith, Tarzan Cooper, John Isaacs, Pop Gates, Pugey Bell, Eyre Saitch, Zack Clayton, Clarence Jenkins.

Abe Saperstein (on ladder) shows some of his Harlem Globetrotters giants "how to shoot a basket."

Nat "Sweetwater" Clifton

95

played only seven games and then went into the service. Cooper would play four years at Boston, averaging almost 10 points a game the first year. He played two more years at Fort Wayne, Indiana, after leaving Boston.

With the subsequent arrival of players like Bill Russell, Wilt Chamberlain, Nate Thurmond, Oscar Robertson, Kareem Abdul-Jabbar, Julius Erving, Magic Johnson and Michael Jordan, blacks have continued to dominate in a sport that denied them for so long.

Amazing Milestones along that path include:

• The first black to lead the NBA in scoring was Wilt Chamberlain, who averaged 37.6 points per game in 1959-60. He retained the title for the next five years.

• The last white scoring leader in the NBA was Jerry West, who averaged 37.2 points in 1969-70.

• The first black coach in professional basketball was John McLendon, who coached the Cleveland Pipers in the short-lived American Basketball League in 1961-62.

• The first black coach in the NBA was Bill Russell, who took over for Red Auerbach in 1966-67 and won the NBA title the next season.

• The first black coach to be fired was Detroit's Earl Lloyd in 1972, which allowed Ray Scott to become the first black coach to succeed another.

• The last all-white team to win an NBA championship was the 1957-58 St. Louis Hawks.

• The first black general manager in the NBA was Wayne Embry, who took over the Milwaukee Bucks in 1976.

• The first NBA championship team to start five blacks was the 1963-64 Celtics with Bill Russell, Sam and K. C. Jones, Satch Sanders and Willie Naulls.

• Black coaches in the NBA now include K. C. Jones at Boston, Bernie Bickerstaff at Seattle, Lenny Wilkens at Cleveland and Bill Russell, newly hired at Sacramento. Black general managers include Wayne Embry at Cleveland and Elgin Baylor with the Los Angeles Clippers. Wes Unseld, another former NBA star, is vice president of the Washington Bullets.

• John Thompson of Georgetown became the first black to coach to win an NCAA division I championship when his Hoyas won the title in 1984.

"Meadowlark" Lemon (right) of the Globetrotters.

FOUR AMAZING INCIDENTS OF RACIAL PREJUDICE

★ The racial prejudice blacks faced was so bad that the University of Tennessee refused to play a scheduled game against Duquesne on December 23, 1946, because Duquesne freshman Chuck Cooper was black.

Duquesne Coach Chick Davies made a conditional promise that Cooper would not see action, but Vols Coach John Mauer still refused to play.

★ Two weeks later the University of Miami cancelled an outdoor game against Duquesne scheduled to be played in the Orange Bowl, citing a city ordinance that prohibited whites and blacks from playing in the same contest.

★ In 1948 the NAIB tournament in Kansas City sought promises from all participating teams that blacks not be allowed to play. Manhattan College, which had no blacks, threatened to pull out, as did Long Island University and Sienna College. The NAIB committee then reversed itself and allowed blacks to play (the NAIB is now the NAIA).

★ The University of Kentucky represented the Southeastern Conference in the NCAA tournament three times in four seasons because Mississippi State refused to play against blacks. In 1958-59, Kentucky was the SEC runner-up, but still received an NCAA bid when the Bulldogs declined it. In 1960-61, they turned down the bid again; UK defeated Vanderbilt in a playoff to determine the SEC representative. In the following year, Kentucky and Mississippi State were co-champions of the league, so the Wildcats again advanced.

Chapter 12
ALMOST HONEST ABE
LEAVES 'EM LAUGHING
Amazing basketball quotes

Once Upon A Time a major-college basketball coach — Abe Lemons, no doubt — stood up before a group of unhappy alumni and said, "Fellas, I know you'd like to have an NCAA championship to brag about, but I've just never been able to get my boys to win one for the Quipper."

Lemons, who has coached at Pan American, Texas, and Oklahoma City, is a man who never won an NCAA championship or lost a banquet.

He's a very funny guy, so we've chosen him as captain of our All-American Quote Team, a solid, fast-talking bunch that can score on or off the court. Here are a few samples from a bag of Lemons.

On comparing coaching to other professions:

"Just once I'd like to see the win-loss records of doctors right out front where people could see them — won ten, lost three, tied two."

On being asked if he jogged:

"Hell no. When I die I want to be sick."

On being compared to a football coach:

"I'd rather be a football coach. That way you can lose only 11 games a season. I lost 11 games in December alone."

On establishing rules for his teams:

"If I make a set of rules, then a guy goes out and steals an airplane. He comes back and says, 'It wasn't on the list of rules.'"

On scheduling opponents:

"I'll give a lecture in a clinic and look for the guy who's taking notes. That's the guy I want to schedule a game with the next year."

On how to stop the evils of recruiting:

"Just give every coach the same amount of money and tell him he can keep what's left over."

On being fired from Texas:

'I looked around the room and nobody else was there, so he had to be talking to me."

However, Lemons isn't the only funny guy in the basketball world. Consider, please, the classic exchange between Atlanta Hawks forward John Drew and a club secretary who was taking information for an insurance form:

Secretary: "What's your birth date, John?"

Drew: "September 30."

Secretary: "What year?"

Drew: "Every year."

Opposite page: Abe Lemons, alias the Quipper, receives a ride from his players after winning the NIT championship game over North Carolina State in 1978.

Here then, assembled in alphabetical order (from A to Z) according to their authors, are 26 amazing basketball quotes and quips, not all of them necessarily uttered by people connected with the game:

"Show me a good loser and I'll show you a loser."
Arnold "Red" Auerbach and Oliver North.

"I really don't like talking about money. All I can say is that the Good Lord must have wanted me to have it."
Larry Bird and Joan Collins.

"I'm getting $300,000 but over a 150-year period."
Denny Crum.

"Because the Brooklyn Bridge wasn't for sale."
Ned Doyle, advertising exec, explaining why he was buying an ABA franchise.

"It's easy once you learn how to fly."
Julius Erving explaining how he dunks.

"We're the only team in history that could lose nine games in a row and then go into a slump."
Bill Fitch, Cleveland Cavaliers/Casey Stengel, New York Mets.

"Happy Days Are Here Again" in Boston, as Red Auerbach and the Celtics sign Larry Bird to his first pro contract.

100

Dr. J., Julius Erving

Pete Maravich

"We'd go back to the motel and wake up Wilt."
Los Angeles Laker guard Gail Goodrich explaining what the team did after 10 a.m. practices on days without a game.

"I don't understand it. How do you expect a $30,000 ballplayer like me to stop a guy who's making $300,000?"
Atlanta Hawk guard Wilbur Holland explaining how Pete Maravich scored 40 points against him.

"It looks like those guys have been sleeping for 20 years."
Washington Irving, author of Rip Van Winkle, discussing the hapless Los Angeles Clippers.

"It's really great being Magic Johnson the basketball player for eight months and then plain Earvin Johnson for the other three."
Magic Johnson expounding on life and the 11-month calendar.

"Hell, I don't even watch the pros. If the NBA was on Channel 5 and a bunch of frogs were making love on Channel 4, I'd watch the frogs — even if they came in fuzzy."
General Bobby Knight discussing his love for professional basketball.

"I never noticed that Bird was white or black. I didn't even know he was human."
Utah Jazz Coach Frank Layden on Larry Bird's abilities vs. skin color.

"Son, looks to me like you're spending too much time on one subject."
Texas A&M Coach Shelby Metcalf to a player who received one D and four F's.

"When a coach is hired, he's fired. The date just hasn't been filled in yet."
Alabama Coach C. M. Newton on the longevity of college basketball coaches.

"People keep coming up to Ralph and asking him if he's Ralph Sampson. I mean, who else could he be?"
Mike Owens, Virginia teammate of Ralph Sampson, on the perception of the average basketball fan.

"Funny, I was about to ask you the same question."
Notre Dame Coach Digger Phelps when asked by alumnus Carl Yastrzemski when his team was ever going to win a championship.

"If I had known the Clippers were this bad I would have stayed with windmills."
Don Quixote, sixth round pick at power forward, on life with the Los Angeles Clippers.

"Young man, you have the question backward."
Majestic Bill Russell when asked how he would have done against Kareem Abdul-Jabbar.

"We're the big brother, they're the little brother."
Kentucky Coach Eddie Sutton giving his opinion of the University of Louisville's relative position in the state.

"I'm not into that business of being relevant to kids. I'm not playing on their team; they're playing on mine. We have certain ways of acting here. My kids are not going to come in here and say, 'Hey baby.' It doesn't make you less of a man to have respect for people."
Georgetown Basketball Coach John Thompson.

"If we just had one big horse in the middle we could whip the Trojans."
Ulysses.

"The time-outs smell a lot better."

New Orleans Coach Bill van Breda Kolff on why he preferred coaching women's basketball.

"I don't know whether always winning is good. It breeds envy and distrust in others and overconfidence and a lack of appreciation very often in those who enjoy it."

UCLA Coach John Wooden, who certainly should have known.

"They all look like cheap imitations of Magic Johnson."

Nova Scotia State Coach L. G. Xerox on the trend of 6-foot-9 kids trying to play guard.

"Nobody goes there anymore, it's too crowded."

Yogi Berra (it would be total sacrilege to not have him somewhere in this list).

"Sometimes it's frightening when you see a 19-year-old kid running down the floor with your paycheck in his mouth."

Bob Zufplatz, a coach at Boston College, on living with 19-year-olds.

John Wooden, the Purdue player and the UCLA coach.

AMAZING QUOTE QUIZ

Now that you've got the hang of this quote business, here's a short quiz on the subject. See if you can identify who said the following:

1. *"I learned a long time ago that minor surgery is when they do the operation on someone else, not you."*
(A) Bernard King   (B) Bill Walton   (C) Ronald Reagan
(D) Kevin McHale   (E) Patrick Ewing.

2. *"If you make every game a life-and-death proposition, you're going to have problems. For one thing, you'll be dead a lot."*
(A) Bobby Knight   (B) Al McGuire   (C) Winston Churchill
(D) Dean Smith   (E) All of Above.

3. He said of the NBA playoffs, *"They just go on and on. It's like a guy telling a bad joke for 15 minutes."*   (A) Red Auerbach
(B) Billy Martin   (C) Tom Heinsohn   (D) Billy Barty
(E) Billy Joel.

4. *"We have a great bunch of outside shooters. Unfortunately, all our games are played indoors."*   (A) Jerry Tarkanian
(B) Weldon Drew   (C) Abe Lemons   (D) Wendell Ladner
(E) George Raveling.

5. *"When you go into a restaurant and the waitresses' ankles are dirty, you know the chili's good."*   (A) Jud Heathcote
(B) Rollie Massimino   (C) Al McGuire   (D) Jim Valvano
(E) Eddie Sutton.

6. *"Be more concerned with your character than with your reputation, because your character is what you really are, while your reputation is merely what others think you are."*   (A) Mother Teresa
(B) Bobby Knight   (C) Adolph Rupp   (D) John Wooden
(E) Jim Bakker.

7. *"My biggest thrill came the night Elgin Baylor and I combined for 73 points in Madison Square Garden. Elgin had 71 of them."*
(A) Jerry West   (B) Norm Nixon   (C) Hot Rod Hundley
(D) Walt Hazzard   (E) Johnny Kerr.

8. *"I don't have an ulcer. I'm a carrier. I give them to other people."*
(A) Red Auerbach   (B) Bill Fitch   (C) Bill Russell
(D) Larry Brown   (E) Hubie Brown.

Al McGuire: "When I was losing, they called me nuts. When I was winning, they called me eccentric."

*University of Kentucky coach
Eddie Sutton.*

QUIZ ANSWERS

1. (B) Bill Walton
2. (D) Dean Smith
3. (C) Tom Heinsohn
4. (B) Weldon Drew
5. (C) Al McGuire
6. (D) John Wooden
7. (C) Hot Rod Hundley
8. (B) Bill Fitch

Chapter 13
WHO'S THE DANCER IN SHORT PANTS?
The amazing struggle of the early pros

ORIGINAL CELTICS

Johnny Beckman

Dutch Dehnert

Joe Lapchick

Nat Holman

Pete Barry

The Original Celtics.

The ink was barely dry on the list of 13 rules for James Naismith's brand-new game before somebody began figuring out how to make a buck from this latest fad in winter sports.

There was no need for agents — yet. Professional basketball would rise and fall during the next century like a hungry kid on a greased pole. Yet its spot at the top was inevitable. There were already too many basketball players with nowhere else to go.

The Doc's game had taken off with phenomenal speed. By 1895 the various YMCAs were already holding regional championships, which inevitably led to a national championship. This in turn led, of course, to overemphasis.

The games became too rough. The fans behaved like gorillas at a church social. This did not fit the general concept of a Young Men's Christian Association, and it wasn't five years after the first YMCA nurtured the game that a few chapters began a nationwide campaign to de-emphasize it.

It was a futile effort: this basketball horse had already been saddled.

The players didn't want to give up the game. Basketball was fun, gave them a little notoriety and fueled their competitive fires. So they dropped off the YMCA circuit, but stayed together as a team, and began looking for other places with peach baskets.

Not even Indiana had 10,000-seat high school gymnasiums in those days. There were few civic auditoriums or arenas. The closest Astrodome was 60 years away. So the old-timers found armories, dance halls, theaters, movie houses, any building that might have room for a couple of portable baskets and 10 guys in short pants.

Basketball was a barely respectable pursuit, if at all. Often the players had to dribble around support poles set in the middle of the floor, or dance around the pot-bellied stove sitting in the corner. They learned to bounce off the netting promoters put around the dance floors to keep the ball in bounds, and how to dodge the hatpins an irate fan might shove through the openings.

Picture, if you can, the game of that era, in dim, cramped dance halls, sometimes with ceilings barely 15 feet over the floor. The players often wore heavy shorts and long-sleeved woolen jerseys. The spectators, in suits, derby hats and handlebar mustaches, cheered lustily, occasionally lighting victory cigars.

The game was a goofy series of short passes, flat-footed rebounding and two-handed shots thrown up by short, muscular men using leather balls with heavy stitches. The whole scene was like some grainy, black-and-white silent movie, only with noise and cigar smoke.

But there was SOMETHING about this game that worked, that made it fun to watch. It appealed to some basic need within all of us to pick up a ball and throw it, preferably at some target, or maybe a basket.

The problem was the players often had to pay rent for these crude arenas. The only way to raise rent money was to stand outside before the game started and sell tickets, or pass the derby afterwards. So professional basketball was born out of selfish necessity, the desire of its pioneers to play at least two out of three games indoors.

Can you imagine Magic Johnson or Michael Jordan having to stand out front of the L. A. Forum selling tickets? And those modern-day superstars surely don't love the game any more than their 19th-century counterparts whose two biggest worries were paying the rent and falling into the orchestra pit.

Very few men could make a living playing basketball in the late 1890s; it was an era when most professional athletes were given all the love and respect of a wino at a Park Avenue wedding.

Basketball historians are split on the location of the first professional basketball game. A few say it was played at the Fox Opera House in Herkimer, N. Y., in 1893. Most claim it was at the Masonic Hall in Trenton, N. J., in 1896, where each player earned $15 from crowd receipts, a handsome sum for the day, and the team captain received $16.

In spite of that heady start, the professional game bounded along in the late 1890s on very unsteady flooring. The better players (and there was great disparity between the good, the bad and the ugly) were like their baseball counterparts; they would often hop from team to team at the sound of a billfold opening.

Every team had its own basketball rules. The team personnel changed nightly. The basketball games were often just sideshows to the dances held on the same floor, and often a highly-polished, 40-foot-by-60-foot floor at that.

Indeed, Dr. Luther Gulick, the very man who dispatched The Doc to invent the game, was quoted in 1898 as saying, ". . . when men commence to make money out of a sport it degenerates with tremendous speed . . . It has inevitably resulted in men of lower character going into the game."

Alas, that admonition was lost on one William Sheffer, who formed the country's first professional basketball league that same year. Called The Philadelphia League, it was formed of teams from such basketball-rabid towns as Trenton, Camden, Philadelphia, Germantown, Hancock and Millville. It died out in 1903.

His idea didn't.

Hot on the flimsy heels of the pro experiment in Philadelphia, the true hotbed of the professional sport in this country, came the Eastern League, which expanded to Reading, Jasper, Princeton, DeNeri and Elizabeth, as well as Trenton. Trenton — with the immortal Harry Hough shooting all its free throws, as was permissible at that time — ran off with the league title.

108

CHAMPIONSHIP BASKETBALL
ORIGINAL CELTICS

CLAIMANTS NATIONAL PROFESSIONAL CHAMPIONSHIP

VS.

KINGSTON STATE LEAGUERS
THURSDAY, FEBRUARY 9

REGULAR
PRICES
—
GAME AT
8:30 P. M.

DANCING
FOLLOWS
GAME

Standing from left to right: Mgr. Frank Morgenweck, "King" Lehr, Harry Knoblauck, Business Mgr. Ed. D. Fitzgerald. Sitting from left to right: Benny Borgmann, Cal' Husta, George Artus, Mike Husta.

The ORIGINAL CELTICS are conceded to be the greatest basketball team of the present day. They have won 78 and lost 3 games this season. Mgr. Turey will bring his regular lineup to Kingston including Johnny Beekman, Nat. Holman, Dutch Dehnert, Chris. Leonard, Tommy Barry, Ernie Reich and Flo. Haggerty.

STATE ARMORY
KINGSTON, N. Y.

LEAGUE GAMES AT KINGSTON ARMORY EVERY TUESDAY

C. M. Thomas' Sons, Classy Printers, Kingston, N.Y.

After that you need a Rand-McNally atlas to keep track of professional basketball. From 1906 through 1926 the various leagues included the Hudson River League, the New York State League, and the Western Pennsylvania League, not to be confused with the Pennsylvania State League.

There was also the Inter-State League, the Metropolitan Basketball League, which indicated the game was at least moving out of DeNeri and Millville, and the more grandly named American Basketball League, born in 1926 and buried a few years later.

For all the attempts at organization, it was still the showy, independent, barnstorming teams of the day that got the most attention. Ed Wachter and his Troy (New York) Trojans had set the Eastern League on fire around 1910

Ed Sullivan

"Master Mind" Doc Tally in 1928, the star of the House of David. His bearded basketball team toured the country, usually playing local squads, sometimes as preliminaries to American Basketball League games.

with new innovations called the bounce pass and the fast break. Wachter, incidentally, was also the guy who promoted the concept that the fouled player should shoot the free throw.

There were occasional stars in other leagues, but mostly the teams, and the players, played within one section of the map, limiting their exposure.

A team that changed all that, and it takes a while to get used to this name, was a mighty quintet called the NEW YORK Celtics.

Some great basketball names just never die.

The New York Celtics began in 1912 in the Hudson Guild Settlement House on New York's lower West Side. The name Celtics was used because the players were in a guild social club of that name. It was already a strong team before World War I, but it was after the war, under new management and renamed the "Original Celtics," that it came back and practically revolutionized basketball.

Pushed through the promotional efforts of a then-sportswriter in New York named Ed Sullivan, who knew a "reeaally big shew" when he saw one, the Celtics barnstormed the East on a 200-games-a-year schedule.

The Celtics played their biggest rival, Tex Rickard's New York Whirlwinds, before 11,000 fans in New York's 71st Regiment Armory in 1921. That was supposed to be the first of a three-game series for the professional championship, except that the two teams split the first two games and, supposedly fearing fan mayhem, never played the third.

It was a little like going home for the winter with the World Series tied at three games apiece because nobody wanted to hire security for the seventh game.

In 1922 the Celtics, the first pro franchise to offer exclusive contracts and guaranteed salaries, solved the rivalry problem by signing the Whirlwinds' two best players. In 1923 the team had 204 wins, 11 losses and, no doubt, very sore feet.

The Celtics were the first team to use the "give and go" offense, pivot plays, and a switching man-to-man defense. They were also as thoroughly hated as they were successful; miners in coal towns were known to wear their head lamps to basketball games to shine in the Celtics' glowering eyes.

Professional basketball made a solid attempt at class and stability in 1925 when George Preston Marshall, a Washington laundry owner who would later own the Washingston Redskins in the National Football League, formed the American Basketball League. Both leagues had so far to go that one man, Joe F. Carr, was president of both the NFL and the ABL.

The Celtics had things pretty much their own way in the unsteady world of professional basketball and refused to join this new league. The ABL, fighting back, prohibited any of its members from playing the Celtics. The

The World Champion Cleveland Rosenblums, who became the Cleveland Rebels when the American Basketball League was formed in 1925.

WORLD'S CHAMPIONSHIP
BASKETBALL
Rosenblum - Celtics
World's Professional Champions
—— VS ——
New York Renaissance
World's Colored Champions

Thurs., Feb. 1   Central Gymn
Evansville, Ind.

Evansville Fans Will See The Greatest Attraction Basketball Can Offer!

Celtics then were forced to join the league to survive and the ABL launched the 1926-27 season with teams in Baltimore, Cleveland, Fort Wayne, New York, Philadelphia, Rochester, Washington and Chicago, a team owned by George Halas before he decided professional football might be a more gentle way to make a living.

In spite of its attempt at class, the ABL had a number of quaint edges to it. The Fort Wayne team was run by the Chamber of Commerce, and the Cleveland team was named the Rosenblums after Max Rosenblum, the department store owner who owned the franchise.

The fighting Rosenblums had a good start that first season, but lost three straight to the Celtics in the playoffs. There were worse losses, however; George Preston Marshall lost $65,000 with his Washington Palace team that first year and dropped from the league.

After being forced to join the ABL, the awesome Celtics repaid everyone the first two years by so dominating the league that attendance dropped. In 1929 the Celtics were broken apart, with the better players being dispersed to three different teams. It didn't matter; five of the old Celtics eventually ended up with the Rosenblums and they ran off with the league title.

So in 1931 the league owners then shot themselves in the basketball shoe with one of the dumbest rules of all time: they mandated each team had to play at least two "inexperienced" (weaker) players at all times.

The ABL won the victory, but lost the war; the Rosenblums dropped out of the league at mid-season, but the league folded at the end of the year.

Wounded in the foot or not, professional basketball refused to die. A new American League was formed in 1934 with remnants of teams from the Metropolitan League and the Eastern League. In 1937 Lonnie Darling, promoter of the Oshkosh All-Stars, organized a National League of midwestern teams.

As those teams crawled toward the 1940s and World War II, five members of the Original Celtics bought a second-hand Pierce-Arrow for $125 and went back to touring the country for a guaranteed $125 a game or 60 percent of the gate, whichever was higher.

AMAZING FACTS ABOUT CAGES

The Armory Cage, Patterson, New Jersey, is an example of the netting around early basketball courts to keep the ball and players inbounds. This cage was the site of American Basketball League games 1919 - 1933.

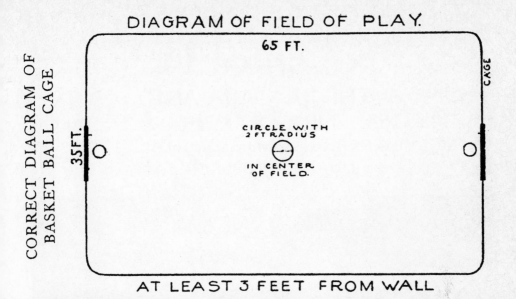

CORRECT DIAGRAM OF
BASKET BALL CAGE

65 FT.

35FT.

CIRCLE WITH
2 FT RADIUS

IN CENTER
OF FIELD.

CAGE

AT LEAST 3 FEET FROM WALL

From the Reach Official Book of Basketball Rules, 1903-04 as played by the National League of Professional Basket Ball Teams of the United States.

RULE I.
The Floor.

All National League championship games must be played in a hall sufficiently large (and clear of posts or other obstructions) to allow of the placing of a cage of the regulation size. Slippery floors must be rosined on demand of either team's captain.

RULE II.
The Cage.

The cage must be sixty-five feet long and thirty-five feet wide. The wire screen must be no less than eleven feet from the floor up and be kept in good repair. The corners of the cage must be round (under no circumstance can a floor be more than five feet short in either length or width, and then only by two-thirds vote of Managers). Should any Manager find it compulsory to complain to President that any cage is in poor condition he (the President) should order Secretary to write to said Manager to repair said cage before the next League game, which order must be obeyed or said Manager fined for negligence.

RULE III.
Light.

The playing space must be illuminated to the satisfaction of the referee, and should any of the floors be poorly illuminated and complaint made by visiting Manager, the President should order the negligent Manager to better light up said floor or be fined at least twenty-five dollars ($25.00) for neglecting to do so when ordered by the President.

Chapter 14
THE BAA, ABA AND NBA ON CBS
Professional basketball's amazing growth

You have to know that any organization named The Basketball Association of America wouldn't last. The name was too dull. The initials — BAA — just didn't make it. Watching the BAA on CBS just doesn't have the same ring as watching the NBA on CBS.

But the BAA is where the NBA began. The date was June 6, 1946. World War II was over, the soldiers were home, and the sports boom had begun. College basketball was growing up and its stars were looking for a bigger house.

The eleven charter members of the Basketball Association of America were the Boston Celtics (you know where that nickname came from), the Chicago Stags (without George Halas), the Cleveland Rebels, the Detroit Falcons, the New York Knickerbockers, the Philadelphia Warriors, the Pittsburgh Ironmen, the Providence Steamrollers, the St. Louis Bombers, the Washington Capitols and, with a brief nod toward The Doc, the Toronto Huskies.

This was a big-time loop. The reason was simple. The BAA was put together by men already associated with large arenas in the major cities. That included Ned Irish, representing the New York Knickerbockers, who was already making a mint with his college doubleheaders at Madison Square Garden.

Irish, in fact, only got into the pro game to be sure the new league wouldn't blindside his billfold. Many of the other BAA founders also booked hockey, and the Sonja Henie ice show. The owners wanted to try professional basketball to keep their arenas filled. They already knew about publicity, crowd control, scheduling and making money, so why not try pro basketball?

The down side was that the National League, with its teams in Rochester, Fort Wayne, Syracuse, Indianapolis, Oshkosh, Sheboygan, Anderson, Toledo, Youngstown, Moline, Detroit and Chicago was still in operation. So was the American League, an eastern professional circuit with teams in Philadelphia, Baltimore, Pittsburgh, Akron, Wilmington and New York.

Competition for the players and the fans was fierce. It eased somewhat when most of the American League teams, for financial and geographic reasons, melted into the BAA. However, the National League — with the top name in the game, Chicago's George Mikan — controlled many of the best college players. The two leagues were soon locked in a recruiting war, with the better-paid players able to command a princely $6,000 a year.

After only one year in the BAA, Cleveland, Detroit, Pittsburgh and Toronto (sorry, Doc) folded for financial reasons. The league added Baltimore and struggled through the 1947-48 season with eight teams, four in each division.

Opposite page: George Mikan is shown in 1947 as the leader of the NBL's Chicago American Gears. Mikan was the NBA's first dominating "big man" and he was voted the Greatest Player of the First-Half-Century by the Associated Press.

The BAA and the National League, where Mikan was now playing for Minneapolis, continued their financial arm-wrestling. The match was something of a standoff because the BAA had the big-city arenas, but the National had a little more money and most of the stars.

Maurice Podoloff, the five-foot-tall president of the BAA, saw that the only answer was a merger. He worked on the owners of the Fort Wayne Pistons and the mighty Indianapolis Jets. He convinced them professional basketball belonged in the big cities like New York and Boston. He sold them on the prestige of life in large arenas. It worked. Fort Wayne and Indianapolis jumped to the BAA. Minneapolis, with Mikan, and Rochester, the other National League powerhouse, soon followed.

So the BAA had twelve teams in 1948-49, including Mikan, the biggest draw in the game. In 1949-50 it was a simple step to add most of the remaining National League teams to the BAA and rename the whole league . . . trumpets please . . . The National Basketball Association.

It was a fine name with great promise. The NBA was also a league of 17 teams stretched from Denver to New York. It was too big and unwieldy, but at least it had no other major leagues to contend with. Yet.

The 17 teams didn't last long. In the next few years the NBA dropped to 11 teams, and then eight. The public stayed away in droves from a game that was often crude, rough and boring. In a November 22, 1950, game between Fort Wayne and Minneapolis, both teams stalled as the fans pelted the players and referees with abuse and debris. Fort Wayne finally won, in the lowest-scoring contest in NBA history, 19-18. Because of stalling, and the trading of fouls to get the ball back, the finish of one NBA playoff game wasn't even seen on national television. It lasted more than three hours, so the network just pulled the plug and went home.

In 1954 Danny Biasone, owner of the Syracuse team, offered a solution.

Maurice Podoloff

Abe Saperstein

He proposed a rule that a team must shoot within 24 seconds or lose the ball. It was the salvation of the game.

Other leagues formed to compete with the NBA. In 1961, Abe Saperstein, whose Harlem Globetrotters often shared the bill with professional teams and were a much better draw, became angry with NBA owners for denying him a franchise in Los Angeles. He formed the short-lived American Basketball League with eight teams, often propped up by appearances of his Globetrotters. Money in Saperstein's ABL was so scarce that teams traveling to Honolulu, one of the league's cities, would play the Hawaii Chiefs four or five nights in a row to save on airfare. The arrangement was good for suntans but bad for the league. The ABL died in 18 months, leaving Saperstein about $2 million poorer. Its lasting legacy was the novel idea that an especially long shot — 25 feet in the ABL — should be worth three points.

The American Basketball Association was founded in 1967, a better-funded organization with announced teams in New York, Anaheim, Pittsburgh, Houston, Kansas City, New Orleans, Minneapolis, Dallas, Oakland, Indianapolis, and Louisville. It adopted the ABL's three-point shot, a red, white and blue basketball, and a 30-second clock.

The ABA, like all professional leagues before it, had all the stability of a Central American bank. Yet it hung on, attracted prominent players like Artis Gilmore, Louie Dampier, Dan Issel and Julius Erving, and battled the NBA for almost 10 years. In time, as with the BAA and the National League 25 years earlier, the better ABA franchises went into the NBA. The rest disappeared.

Meanwhile, in the NBA, Red Auerbach had built his Boston team into a perennial champion. The awesome Celtics won 11 of 13 championships from 1957 to 1969, including eight in a row, a dynasty unmatched in any professional sport. Auerbach finally retired from coaching after the eight straight wins (with a 938-479 overall coaching record) and he handed the team to Bill Russell. Red moved upstairs to light victory cigars, as Russell added two more championship banners to the Boston Garden ceiling.

Since 1969, however, no team has repeated for the NBA title, even though in six of the last seven years Boston or Los Angeles has won the title.

Professional basketball still has its problems, but the weaker teams draw about 8,000 fans a game, the better teams from 14,000 to 17,000 a game, and television ratings continue to rise. It has come a long way from the nights when players earned $15 a game and couldn't believe their luck.

By 1987-88 there were 23 NBA franchises, with expansion looming. The NBA playoffs appear coast-to-coast on prime-time television and no network would dare pull the plug.

119

A FEW MORE AMAZING STORIES
FROM PROFESSIONAL BASKETBALL

• Contrary to what you might think, Red Auerbach was not born in a cloud of cigar smoke beneath the parquet floor of Boston Garden. In fact, Auerbach coached the Washington Capitols in the old BAA for three seasons. During 1948-49, despite a fine won-lost record, he quit in an administrative dispute and took a job as an "advisory coach" at Duke University that fall.

Auerbach was unhappy in the college game when he received an offer to coach — can you believe this? — the Tri-Cities team in Moline, Illinois. The Tri-Cities — Rock Island, Moline and Davenport — had just joined the NBA. In six weeks Auerbach completed deals involving 28 players. He led his cornfield kids into the playoffs, lost to the eventual league runner-up, and then quit in another managerial dispute.

The next year, before the 1950-51 season, Auerbach went to work for Walter Brown in Boston. It took him six years and Bill Russell to build a winner.

• Only the New York Knicks and the Boston Celtics remain from the original NBA franchises. Some of the original towns still have teams, but the franchises have changed over the years. For example, Red Auerbach's Tri-City Hawks became the Milwaukee Hawks the following year, then the St. Louis Hawks, and now the Atlanta Hawks.

• Dating back to 1947 with the old BAA, a total of 59 teams have played in the league. The extinct include the Anderson (Indiana) Packers and the Providence Steamrollers.

• Bill Willoughby became the youngest player in NBA history when he took the floor for the Atlanta Hawks at age 18 years, 5 months, 3 days. The oldest player was Bob Cousy, who appeared in a game at 41 years, 6 months and 2 days, although Kareem Abdul-Jabbar, who will be 41 on April 16, 1988, might catch him.

• Some of the more inspired team nicknames from the old ABA were the San Diego Conquistadors, the San Diego Sails, the Pittsburgh Condors, the Pittsburgh Pipers and the Minnesota Muskies. There were 28 different teams — or at least team names — in the ABA.

• How rotten was the shooting in the old-time basketball games? In the 1946-47 season, Bob Feerick of the Washington Capitols led the league with a .401 shooting percentage. Feerick never had it so good; a year later he led the league with a .340 shooting percentage!

120

• How rotten was the shooting by 1960? Wilt Chamberlain hauled down 55 rebounds in one game in 1960 and Bill Russell had 51 in a game the same year. No one in professional basketball ever hit more than 50 percent of his shots until Chamberlain dropped in 50.7% in the 1960-61 season. The league-leading percentage has never been below 50 percent since.

Wilt hit an amazing 72.7% in 1972-73, the all-time NBA record.

Bob Cousy (left) and coach Red Auerbach (right) of the Boston Celtics, make a toast with owner Walter Brown. The Celtics were celebrating their fifth straight world championship.

As you can see in the accompanying photograph, there has always been a close working relationship between the cheerleader and the referee. One or the other is always on the floor, each wears a distinctive uniform designed to accommodate creature comfort as well as instant recognition, and both can incite a near-riot at the slightest wave of a hand.

It's always been that way for referees, who have accumulated fewer friends over the last century than cholera. Yet The Doc realized early on that his game had to have impartial arbiters, and he incorporated them in rules ten and eleven of his Original 13:

RULE 10: The umpire shall be judge of the men and shall note fouls and notify the referee when three consecutive fouls have been made. He shall have power to disqualify men . . .

RULE 11: The referee shall be judge of the ball and shall decide when the ball is in play, in bounds, to which side it belongs and shall keep the time. He shall decide when a goal has been made, and keep account of the goals . . .

You can see the problems. With the original rules, only one person, the umpire, was responsible for calling fouls. It was important for the umpire to note consecutive fouls because in basketball's earliest days if a team collected three straight fouls, the other team was awarded a goal. And some of those early teams had 10 to 15 men on a side. It would have been easier to count gunshots at the OK Corral.

The referee seemed to have the better of the deal in the early game. All he had to do was keep the ball in play, decide when the ball went into the peach basket, and keep score.

The original scoring, incidentally, awarded three points for both a basket and a free throw. The rules were changed to allow two points for a basket and one point for a free throw for the 1895-96 season.

For a few brief years a second umpire was added to call fouls, but that practice quickly died out. In 1895 a "secretary" was added to the off-court bureaucracy to perform scorekeeper and time-keeper duties, and a year later the referee was actually allowed to call fouls if the umpire missed one. At that time the umpire was chosen by the visiting team, the referee was chosen by the home team and neither was allowed to question the call of the other. There were probably a lot of games when they left under separate police escorts, too.

It wasn't until 1929, almost 40 years after basketball was invented, that two floor officials with nearly identical duties became commonplace, although many colleges regularly used two officials long before that.

Opposite page: Cindy Acker, cheerleader for the Floridians basketball team of the ABA, tries to get a look at some of the action on the court over the shoulder of referee Mark Schlafman.

What a 40 years that was. No two parts of the country used the same basketball rules or standards for fouls. In some of the smaller gymnasiums and dance halls, local options allowed the players to bounce the ball off the walls and ceilings. In gymnasiums where the backboard was attached to the wall, a player might leap against the wall, then spring upward toward the basket to shoot, or even dunk.

Many of those buildings had roof supports in the middle of the floor, or coal-burning stoves in the corners, adding to the charm if not the floor burns. Many coaches devised plays to have their opponents bounced off pillar and post as part of the offense. It wasn't until 1903-04 that the boundaries around the court were required to be straight lines, and before that there were often no boundaries at all. It wasn't until the 1916-17 season that the end walls were decreed to be out of bounds, ending the leaping, off-the-wall, dunk shot.

Before 1917 basketball officials generally wore the handiest items in the clothes closet, none of which came with the convict stripes we often assign to referees today.

Kentucky legend Adolph Rupp, who refereed many games in basketball's early days, said the lack of an official referees' uniform often caused problems.

"I'd just grab an old pair of pants and a shirt, usually white or blue," said Rupp. "Sometimes my shirt was the same color as a team's jersey and I'd be ducking a lot of passes."

As early as 1900 coaches and administrators were complaining about the scarcity of good, consistent referees, a cry that is occasionally heard even today among the nation's calm, competent, chair-throwing coaches.

A few training programs were begun, but the battle for consistent refereeing was hopeless until 1934 when, for the first time, the rules of basketball were standardized coast-to-coast. That didn't eliminate all the problems — even today referees will still allow a much rougher brand of basketball in one area than another — but at least everyone was playing the same game.

In the 1940s college basketball officials began to form organizations to help monitor and train referees, a concept that has since spread to high school, international and professional organizations. In recent years college basketball has added a third official to the game. While meeting with mixed reviews from the coaches, this at least gives them another striped shirt for target practice.

Professional basketball also suffered with uninformed, inconsistent, incompetent refereeing for much of its early years. It wasn't until the 1967-68 season that NBA referees were given contracts; prior to that they were paid from game to game, which wasn't a great way to insure quality or quantity.

In 1977 NBA referees, perhaps noting that the average NBA player's salary was $109,000 a year while referees were earning an average of $26,000 plus

$27 a day in expenses, went on strike during the last day of the season. The NBA responded by holding the playoffs with "scab" referees for 16 days, and then by giving the referees a $150-a-game pay raise.

One early NBA referee who did set some standards rarely equalled in the modern game was Chuck Solodare. In a game at Fort Wayne, Indiana, in the embryonic years of the NBA, Solodare was the target of an exceptional amount of abuse, even by NBA standards. So just before the game was completed Solodare stopped the action, pulled an uncooked steak from his shirt and heaved it up in the stands.

"Here, you wolves," he bellowed. "Chew on that for awhile."

These days the near-incitement to riot is more the responsibility of the cheerleader than the referee. Cheerleading actually pre-dates basketball,

Laying down on the job — ABA referee Norm Drucker, right, prepares to get up after spilling into the stands during playoff action between the New York Nets and Virginia Squires in 1971.

going back to the time when the Romans would leave town to sack another village to the cheering throngs who would scream:

Julius, Julius he's our man
If he can't do it
Nobody can.

Organized cheerleading began in the United States in the 1870s, mostly at football games. The earliest known cheer was the famous "Princeton locomotive." Thousands of Princeton students, apparently of their own accord, would stand and cheer:

Ray, Ray, Ray
Tiger, Tiger, Tiger
Sis, Sis, Sis
Boom, Boom, Boom
Aaaaaaaaaaaaah
Princeton, Princeton, Princeton

You could be sure there wasn't a dry eye in the house when that little beauty was completed.

One of the first yells originated by a student was the emotional "Wah-hoo-wah" introduced by D. A. Rollins, Dartmouth class of 1879.

Johnny Campbell, a student at the University of Minnesota, is generally given credit for leading the first organized cheerleading on a college campus.

Campbell, flushed with pride, would stand before a Minnesota football crowd and shout:

RAH RAH RAH!
SKU-U-MAH,
HOO-RAH
HOO-RAH
VARSITY! VARSITY!
MINN-E-SO-TAH

The invention of basketball, along with the invention of the megaphone, soon moved all this emotion indoors, where college basketball crowds could stand and shout SKU-U-MAH.

Cheerleading, strangely enough, was an all-male endeavor until the 1920s. when schools began letting girl cheerleaders shout SKU-U-MAH in public, a dubious first step in women's battle for equality. About that time, and Minnesota was again the leader, cheerleaders began to incorporate gymnastics and tumbling into their routines.

As basketball evolved, so did cheerleading. The cheers became more sophisticated, cheerleading workshops were begun and in the 1960s, another landmark decade in cheerleading, Fred Gasthoff invented the vinyl pom pom.

Cheerleading in the 1980s now incorporates gymnastics, ballet, weight-lifting, modern dance, muscular choreography, high-fashion design, sexy routines, tumbling, and, if the occasion calls for it, cheers.

High-intensity cheerleading camps and contests for high schools and colleges are held coast-to-coast, with the very best going for the gold on national television. In many big-time basketball schools the cheerleaders are backed by sophisticated, high-energy dance groups that work as hard as any basketball team.

The cheers have kept pace, too. One selection, taken from thousands in a modern-era cheerleading book, goes:

Heaven help the other team
Eagle men are tough and mean.
Go gettum-uh uh-go-gettum.

MORE AMAZING REFEREE AND CHEERLEADING STUFF!

1. The "Princeton locomotive" was born in the Civil War when a group of Princeton undergraduates gathered at the local New Jersey railroad station to watch the Seventh Regiment march off to war. A "rouser" with the regiment began the cheer, and the college boys picked it up.

2. Tommy Canterbury, a Centenary College basketball coach, is credited with the most famous line ever about referees: "The trouble with officials is they just don't care who wins."

Concern and hope are reflected on the faces of two Illinois high school cheerleaders.

Chapter 16
ANYBODY HERE
SPEAK RUSSIAN?
An amazing 63-year losing streak ends

The disputed shot by Alexander Belov wins the 1972 Munich Olympics.

Basketball, as you have surmised by now, is a game that insists on making full circles. A basket was originally worth three points, and now the three-point shot is back with us. For one brief moment in the early game there were three referees, and now they are back with us. So it should be no surprise that the first international basketball game was in 1909 between the two fiercest rivals of the modern era — the United States and the Soviet Union.

The sad news was, the Russians won.

And the obvious evidence from the 1987 Pan American games is that although the United States invented the game, we no longer own it. If an American team can lose to a Brazilian team in a game played in Indiana, it can lose anywhere.

The 1909 contest, played between a touring YMCA team from the States and the Mayak Club of St. Petersburg (now Leningrad), is a perfect example of how amazingly fast basketball traveled around the world from Springfield, Massachusetts.

The reason was the long arms of the YMCA. As dozens of eager young men left its training school for jobs around the world, they took The Doc's game with them. Basketball moved in 1893 to France, where it was played with great elan in the new gymnasium of the Paris YMCA in the Rue de Trevise. In 1893 a Springfield disciple took the game to Tientsin, China, and into India. By 1900 two Far Eastern exchange students had introduced the game to Japan and Persia.

The Russians joined the schedule because the Mayak Club had invited a U. S. citizen, Eric Moraller, to become its physical education director. He introduced basketball there, even outfitting the Russians in the exact same uniforms worn by the students at Springfield College.

Alas, Moraller did his job too well. After one year Mayak had four teams which were playing a regular intramural schedule. In 1909 they invited the Americans over and whipped them at their own game.

That injustice was just a prelude to what would happen to the Americans at the 1972 Olympics.

Within 30 years the Springfield alumni, with 70 YMCAs around the world, had spread basketball from Baghdad to Borneo. Basketball first appeared on the Olympic scene as a "demonstration" sport at the 1904 Olympics held in St. Louis. The winner was a team from Buffalo, N. Y., with a decidedly international name, the Buffalo Germans, but basketball didn't really gain full status until the 1936 Olympics.

World War I, a thoroughly bleak period in most respects, did allow the American Expeditionary Forces to take basketball further into Europe and the Baltic countries. One of the better-informed messengers just happened to be James Naismith, a YMCA employee in France.

In 1927 the World Committee of YMCAs, with the help of Springfield College, established the International School of Physical Education in Geneva, Switzerland. In 1932 this school organized the first international basketball body, the International Amateur Basketball Federation.

This little group couldn't have popped up soon enough. Basketball around the world, like basketball in the States, had evolved in a dozen different directions. Some countries still played the game exactly as The Doc had written it; some had developed their own rules to allow for local conditions and/or stray cattle.

In 1928 Kansas coach Phog Allen had been dispatched to the Olympics in Amsterdam to lobby loudly for basketball to be included as a "demonstration" sport in the 1932 Los Angeles Olympics. Allen received support from other countries, but the California contingent instead voted for a football game, saying it would draw more spectators. So the Germans, with Adolph Hilter pulling all the strings, hosted the first official Olympic basketball games in Berlin in 1936.

The American team, as was often the case in the early years, was chosen from the Amateur Athletic Union (AAU) basketball players. The AAU supervised the game then. It held national championships before the NIT and NCAA were invented, often hosting matches between college, club and company-sponsored teams.

(In 1916 Utah became the first college to win a national AAU championship. In 1920 NYU beat Rutgers in the first all-college final. From the 1930s to the 1960s, company-sponsored teams, such as the Phillips Oilers and the Akron Goodyears, were among the strongest teams in the country, including the pros.)

In the 1930s and 1940s the United States did not hold mass tryouts to select players for our various Olympic, Pan American and world teams. These Olympic teams came from the best AAU or college teams of the day, often after they had met in special, pre-Olympic competition. Our 1936 Olympic squad came mostly from the Universal Pictures and Globe Refining AAU teams.

There were 22 basketball teams at the 1936 Olympics, but Spain had to return home before the action began due to civil war action at home. The Berlin games were played outdoors on a tennis court made of brick, dust, sawdust and salt. The United States sloshed to a 19-8 victory over Canada in the finals during a rainstorm. It was raining so hard that one American fast break was stopped because the ball stuck in the mud during mid-dribble.

World War II somewhat interrupted the Olympic spirit in 1940 and 1944, but, as during World War I, it also gave Americans a chance to promote basketball around the world. The international game started to regroup at the 1948 Olympics, when 22 lesser teams competed against the powerful American squad composed mostly of the Phillips Oilers and the University of Kentucky's "Fabulous Five." The Americans had one close game out of eight, a two-point victory over Argentina, and fried the French in the finals, 65-21, for the gold medal.

The Russian Bear lumbered onto the Olympic scene for the first time at the Helsinki games in 1952. This time the American team was built around players from the Peoria Cats and the University of Kansas. The Russian team was built around borscht and dull basketball. They tried to beat the Americans with a stall, but put everybody to sleep while losing in the finals, 36-25.

Borrrrringgggg — Borrrrringgggg!

In 1956 the Russkies sent out 7-foot 2-inch, 340-pound Ivan "The Terrible" Krouminch against Bill Russell. Ivan was terrible, Russell shut him out, and the Americans won 89-55.

It was more of the same in 1960, 1964, and 1968. This brings us, regrettably, to the 1972 Olympics in Munich, the worst American moment in the history of basketball.

The 1948 U. S. Olympic basketball champions posing in London.

131

The Americans, playing poorly but with a 63-game Olympic winning streak on the line, had finally moved ahead of the Russians 50-49 with three seconds left, on two foul shots by Doug Collins.

The Russians tried to put the ball back in play, and then called time out with only one second showing on the clock. They protested the clock was wrong, and somehow the clock was put back to three seconds.

When play resumed, the Russian inbounds pass was deflected, and time ran out. Victory — albeit a nervous victory — for America.

But wait! A referee argued the ball had not been properly put in play, a decision backed by Robert Jones, secretary-general of the International Amateur Basketball Federation.

Again the clock was set to three seconds. This time the Russians threw a long pass to Alexander Belov, who was standing under the American basket,

The first international championship basketball team, led by Hall of Famer Max "Marty" Friedman (holding the ball). It overwhelmed over 600 teams of servicemen in Paris, 1919.

double-teamed by Kevin Joyce and James Forbes. All three jumped for the ball, but Joyce and Forbes were knocked to the floor. Suddenly it was apparent what was going to happen. Belov, almost in slow motion, laid the ball into the basket. The Russians' 63-year losing streak against America was over.

It was a defeat that still rankles America. All protests were disallowed and the referees, a Brazilian and a Bulgarian, signed the scoresheets. Russia had the gold. The United States, in protest, refused to accept the silver medals.

The U. S. hasn't lost another Olympic game.

The Pan American games proved to be another matter. The Brazilian team, led by the amazing shooting of a hotdog forward named Oscar Schmidt, legitimately beat the American team 120-115 in the 1987 finals in Indianapolis. It was only the third loss ever for a U. S. Pan American team, and the first since 1971. It was, a little ironically, three-point shots that beat the Americans.

The U. S. women, however, beat Brazil 111-87 in the 1987 finals to win their sixth gold medal in nine tries.

The American game of basketball spread quickly across Europe. Here an unidentified man demonstrates the dunk shot to about 25 fascinated village children and two adults.

133

Not even the dangers of war could keep this American Marine from taking a few shots with his trusty basketball and portable buckets.

MORE AMAZING INTERNATIONAL FACTS

★ It is almost impossible to believe how poorly some of the early stars of the game shot the basketball. In the 1952 Olympic finals between the United States and Russia, the Americans hit only 7 of 32 shots the first half, and 13 of 65 for the game. The Russians hit 6 of 22 the first half, and then cooled off to 2 for 22 the second half, or 8 of 44 for the game.

★ The 1948 Olympics marked the first time teams were allowed to use more than five players and five substitutes. As a result, all 14 Americans played against the French during the 65-21 rout in the finals. Only Kentucky's Cliff Barker failed to score.

★ When James Naismith arrived at the 1936 games, the man who had invented basketball learned his name had been stricken from the pass list. It was added after strong arguments by his friends.

★ The 1936 Olympics were played under the rules that existed before 1932. There was no 10-second line and a center jump was held after every made free throw.

★ Only one player on the 1948 U. S. Olympic team, Alex Groza of Kentucky, averaged in double figures (11.1) for the tournament.

★ That same year a diminutive Chinese player, dubbed "Charlie" by the fans, made almost everyone happy when he dribbled between the legs of America's big Bob Kurland and went in for a layup.

★ The 30-second clock started in international play in 1956, mostly as a result of the Russians' Olympic stall against the Americans in 1952.

Chapter 17
WILT AND BEVO
STAND TALL
Fifty amazing firsts

Many fans know that Quinn Buckner was the first man to play on a state championship high school team (Thornridge of Dalton, Illinois, 1972), an NCAA champion (Indiana, 1976), an Olympic champion (Montreal, 1976) and a professional champion (Boston Celtics, 1984).

Here are 49 other Amazing Basketball Firsts:

• Stanford's Hank Luisetti became the first modern-era college player to score 50 points in one game, hitting that total on January 1, 1938, against Duquesne.

• Pete Maravich of LSU became the first and only Division I college player to average at least 40 points a game for three consecutive years, averaging 43.8 as a sophomore, 44.2 as a junior and 44.5 as a senior.

• The first free throw line was 20 feet from the basket! The line was moved to 15 feet in 1894-95.

• University of Arkansas star Tommy Boyer became the first Razorback with one eye to win the NCAA free throw championship. The 6-foot-6-inch Boyer hit 125 of 134 free throws in 1962-63 for a .933 percentage.

• The girls from Ada Byng, Oklahoma, became the first female high school team to win ten state championships, between 1936 and 1976.

• The first televised college basketball game was between Pittsburgh and Fordham in Madison Square Garden on February 28, 1940. Pittsburgh won 50-37. It was also, no doubt, the first game in which the color commentator credited a coach with a "great time-out."

• The first basketball stamp was issued by the Philippines in 1934.

• In 1957 North Carolina became the first (and only) national champion to win in more than one overtime. The Tar Heels finished the year 25 and 0, after upsetting Kansas 54-53 in three overtimes in the NCAA title game.

• A girls' team from Palatka, Florida, became the first high school team to score 100 points while shutting out an opponent, easing past South Jacksonville 108 to 0 on January 22, 1929.

• Abe Saperstein was the first white player to play with the Harlem Globetrotters. He did so because he owned the team, established the schedule, drove the team bus and wanted to save money on another player.

• Wilt Chamberlain became the first (and only) professional player to score 100 points in a game, dropping in 36 (of 63) field goals and 28 (of 32) free throws against the New York Knicks on March 2, 1962. Wilt's Philadelphia team won the defensive struggle, 169-147. The sweetest game of the Dipper's career was played in Hershey, Pa. Wilt hitting 28 of 32 free throws was considered more remarkable than the 100 points.

• The first undefeated college teams were the Nebraska Cornhusker juggernauts of 1898-1900. The teams won 19 games in a row, winning 7 in 1898, 7 in 1899 and 5 in 1900.

Opposite page: Wilt "The Stilt" Chamberlain.

• The University of Louisville was the first college team to win the National Association of Intercollegiate Athletes tournament (1948), the NIT (1956) and the NCAA (1980).

• LeRoy Edwards of Oskosh (Bi'Gosh), Wisconsin, was the first player to win a National Basketball League scoring title and not even average 10 points a game. Edwards averaged 9.0 points per game in 1939-40.

• The first (and only) brothers to each average 40 points a game for a high school season were Bob and Pat Tallent of Maytown High School in Langley, Kentucky. Bob Tallent averaged 40.5 points a game in 1963-64, and Pat Tallent averaged an even 40 points a game in 1970-71.

• The first NBA all-star game was played March 2, 1951, at (where else?) Boston Garden. Some 10,094 people watched the East beat the West 111-94 behind 20 points from "Easy" Ed Macauley. George Mikan, who won the NBA scoring title that season, scored just eight points.

• In 1894 the University of Chicago became the first college to play a full basketball schedule, going 6 and 1, including a 19-11 thrashing of the Chicago YMCA Training School.

• Philadelphia, an historic city for many reasons, was the first town to have its own professional basketball league. The Philadelphia League, including three suburban towns, lasted for three years. Jack Reynolds won the 1904-05 league scoring title, scoring 616 points in 39 games. He did it with

Quinn Buckner.

LeRoy Edwards of the University of Kentucky and Oshkosh.

138

78 baskets and *460 free throws*. The rules at that time allowed one team member to shoot all the free throws.

• In 1954, the DuSable Panthers of Chicago became the first all-black team with a black coach to reach the finals of a state tournament. They lost in the finals to Mt. Vernon, after causing quite a stir.

• St. John's University was the first school to win consecutive NIT tournaments, winning in 1943 and 1944.

• Oklahoma State was the first team to win consecutive NCAA tournaments, winning in 1945 and 1946. Oklahoma State's Bob Kurland became the first player named MVP in the NCAA tournament two years in a row.

• Cheyenne Central (Wyoming) High School became the first high school team to capture 20 state titles, winning 22 between 1926 and 1984, a national record.

• The first professional basketball team located outside the United States was the Toronto Huskies of the Basketball Association of America. The 1946-47 franchise lasted one season.

• The first rules of basketball were governed by the YMCA and the Amateur Athletic Union. The high schools, colleges and professionals did not become involved until later.

• George "The Bird" Yardley became a hero to bald men everywhere by becoming the first professional basketball player to score 2,000 points in a season. Yardley, a skin-headed, slope-shouldered, 6-foot-5, 195-pounder,

Bob Kurland

139

scored 2,001 points for Detroit in the 1957-58 season, breaking George Mikan's record of 1,932.

• Clarence Johnson became the first professional basketball player to be sold to another team when his Baslos Globetrotters sold him to Fond du Lac, Wisconsin, in 1917. No price was given.

• The high-scoring Hobbs, New Mexico, boys' team became the first high school team to average 114 points a game, running up 114.6 points per game in the 1969-70 season. That included a national-record 14 consecutive games over 100 points. In one 1970 game Hobbs beat Roswell 176-49, hitting 81 of 124 field goals and stealing the ball 75 times.

• Frank Selvy of Furman College was the first major college basketball player to score 100 points in a game, hitting that figure in a 149-95 rout of Newberry College in 1954. Fed constantly by his teammates, the Corbin, Kentucky, native had quarters of 24, 13, 25 and 38 points.

• The first American Basketball Association playoff game to draw *less* than 1,000 people was an April 20, 1970 game with the Los Angeles Stars hosting Dallas. An enthralled 971 spectators watched the contest. The Stars drew 8,233 fans in the final game of that playoff series, but moved to Utah the next year anyway.

• Pasadena City (California) College won the first National Junior College Athletic Association Men's Basketball Championship in 1945 and Temple (Texas) Junior College won the first women's title in 1975.

• The first high school boy to score 100 points in a game was Dick Bogenrife of Midway High School in Sedalia, Ohio. Bogenrife went over with authority, scoring 120 points in a game on February 6, 1953. It's still the third highest boys' prep total.

• Christian Steinmetz of the University of Wisconsin became the first college player to score more than 1,000 points in his career. He played from 1903 to 1905.

• Connie Hawkins became the first modern-era player to lead a professional league in scoring without going to college. Barred from Iowa because of his alleged affiliation with gamblers — later disproven — he led the ABA in scoring in the 1967-68 season.

• Centralia (Illinois) is the winningest team in high school basketball history. In 1982 it became the first high school team to win 1500 games.

• Clarence "Bevo" Francis became the first and only basketball legend out of tiny Rio Grande College in Ohio by scoring 113 points against Hillsdale College in 1953, still the national record against a four-year school. The 6-foot 9-inch Francis had scored 116 points against Ashland (Kentucky) Junior College a year earlier. He'd gotten into Rio Grande, which had 94 students, despite having a wife, a son and no high school diploma. In 1953-54 Francis

140

averaged 46.5 points a game against very weak competition, played professional basketball very briefly, and then disappeared.

• Kenneth Johnson of Grandfield, Oklahoma, became the first prep player to ever launch more than 80 shots in one game, taking 85 in a game against Terral, Oklahoma, on January 1, 1979. He made 45 before going home, no doubt to ice his arm.

• Greg Procell became the first (and only) high school player to score more than 3,000 points in a season, scoring 3,173 points in 1969-70 for Noble Ebarb in Louisiana.

• Nate "Tiny" Archibald was the first NBA guard to score more than 1,000 field goals in a season, hitting 1,028 shots for Kansas City-Omaha during the 1972-73 season.

• Jerry Lucas was the first player ever to be named All-American three years in high school (at Middletown, Ohio) and three years in college, at Ohio State. Freshmen were not eligible in those days.

• The first tie in college basketball history occurred on February 9, 1918. Due to an official scorer's error, Kentucky tied Kentucky Wesleyan 21-21.

Bevo Francis and Coach Newt Oliver

Christian Steinmetz

Bud Grant

- The first college basketball doubleheader was played before 16,188 fans in Madison Square Garden on December 29, 1934. New York University beat Notre Dame 25-18 and Westminster beat St. John's 37-33.
- Professional basketball first began playing four 12-minute quarters in 1946. It was done because the college game was then four 10-minute quarters and the professionals wanted to provide more entertainment.
- The first man to play in the NBA and coach a team to football's Super Bowl was Bud Grant. He played for the Minneapolis Lakers in the NBA from 1949 through 1951; his Vikings reached the Super Bowl four times.
- The first national collegiate post-season championship was not the NIT or the NCAA, but the NAIA tournament. Central Missouri won the first championship, beating Morningside of Iowa 35 to 24 on March 12, 1937. James Naismith presented the trophy, named in honor of his wife Maude.
- Nancy Lieberman of Old Dominion became the first woman to play in a men's professional game on June 10, 1986, when she played three minutes for Springfield of the U. S. Basketball League.
- The first male high school prepster to score more than 55 baskets in a game was Johnny Morris of Portsmouth, Va. He dropped in 57, the national record, in a game on February 22, 1961. He scored 127 points, second only to Danny Heater's 135.
- The first ABA game was played on October 13, 1967, with the Oakland Oaks hosting the Anaheim Amigos. Oakland won 134-129. Oakland's Willie Porter scored the first basket with 1:04 gone in the game.
- The first NIT tournament was held in Madison Square Garden in 1938. The first NCAA finals were played in Evanston, Illinois, in 1939.
- The first scoreless prep game in history was played in March, 1925, between two Fargo, North Dakota, girls' teams, Kansal and Pingree. After a scoreless game and three scoreless overtimes the referees flipped a coin. Kansal called heads, won, and Pingree went home a total loser.

1909 ad in The Springfield Daily Republican.

Chapter 18
SPRINGFIELD
100 YEARS LATER
The amazing Hall of Fame

The most popular attraction in the Naismith Memorial Basketball Hall of Fame is the "Shoot-Out." Here visitors can test their accuracy at different heights and distances, while on a moving sidewalk.

Visitors to the new, state-of-the-art, hands-on Basketball Hall of Fame that rises triumphantly above an expressway in downtown Springfield, Massachusetts, are given only a brief glimpse of the struggle it took to get it there.

It's just too much fun touring the hundreds of exhibits, watching the movie "Hoopla" and television clips from old college and professional games, looking at evocative, black-and-white photos of players and teams long forgotten, and firing up a few jump shots from a moving sidewalk.

The move to build this basketball showplace began in 1936. By that time, basketball had already acquired so much history that people began looking around for a place to store it. The only logical place was where it all began — in Springfield.

That move received a big push from the National Association of Basketball Coaches (NABC). The coaches, wanting to honor James Naismith as well as his game, held a few meetings in the late 1930s to discuss fund raising, but all plans were stalled as the nation faced the coming of World War II.

In 1949, John Bunn, a former pupil of The Doc at Kansas and a man who would later become basketball coach at Springfield College, urged the NABC to revive the hall of fame project. Its first home, although not yet a museum, was a little red house next to the Springfield College football field.

Edward J. Hickox, basketball coach at Springfield before Bunn took over, was the hall's first executive secretary. It was a wonderful title, but Hickox served 14 years without a salary, saying the honor of the job was enough. He served with the steady help of Ruth Silva, who was with the hall 27 years as assistant treasurer and assistant director.

Even without a building suitable to house a museum, and without visitors to see it, the Basketball Hall of Fame began inducting members in 1959. Three of the members in that first class were James Naismith, Dr. Luther Gulick and Amos Alonzo Stagg, the trio who had been there at the very beginning.

In 1961, when Springfield College held a Basketball Commemoration Day 100 years after Naismith's birth, a cornerstone was laid on a proposed $860,000 building on the college campus. Attempts were made to raise money nationwide, including solicitations from college coaches and players, but a year later, when excavation work was completed, only $165,000 had been raised.

Nor did money pour into Springfield from grateful coaches and appreciative jump-shooters across the nation; five years after excavation had begun there was still nothing to show for the Basketball Hall of Fame but a big hole in the ground. On February 17, 1968, seven years after the cornerstone was laid, a modest $650,000 building was open to the public.

The Buffalo Germans, who were elected to the Hall of Fame in 1961. Their victories included the 1902 Pan American Games and the exhibition basketball tournament at the 1904 Olympics in St. Louis.

It served for 17 years, but the complaints were that it was too inaccessible to the public, it didn't have the space to do justice to the great game of basketball, and many of its exhibits were lackluster or incomplete.

The hall had wanted to expand all those years, but barely had enough money to stay afloat where it was. That changed in 1978 when some Springfield business leaders approached the hall with an idea that would benefit everyone: why not build a new museum downtown?

In 1980 the state of Massachusetts gave a $5 million grant for the project. The state added an additional $3 million in 1982, and by then a separate Hall of Fame capital campaign was up to $3.4 million. On March 14, 1984, ground was broken for the new hall. On June 30, 1985, the three-level Basketball Hall of Fame was open to the public. Among the inductees that year were Senda Berensen Abbott, Margaret Wade and Bertha Teague, three early coaching giants of the women's game.

The original Hall of Fame on the Springfield campus had seen 630,179 visitors in 17 years. The new Hall of Fame drew 107,836 the first year.

The new hall has an Honors Court where the faces of each of the inductees are enshrined on medallions. The inductees include 71 players, 38 coaches, 42 general contributors to the game and 11 referees. There are also four teams that were taken into the hall intact: Naismith's first Springfield team, the Original Celtics, the Buffalo Germans and the New York Rens.

146

Next to the Honors Court is a large exhibit where basketball history is told in four sections: early development, high school, college, and professional.

The exhibits include old equipment and uniforms, photos of high school stars and a listing of Parade All-American high school teams, life-size pictures of Hall of Fame players in action, and displays featuring the game's great coaches.

There's also a genuine locker room, a section on international basketball and a whole trophy case devoted to the life and times of James Naismith.

The hall also has "Play 52," a basketball movie that's shown on all four walls of the viewing room. As if that isn't enough to get the blood flowing, quadraphonic sound is pumped in from all corners.

Or if you want the real thing, Springfield also plays host to a tip-off game in November of each year featuring two of the best teams in college basketball.

Michael Jordan's locker at the Hall of Fame.

Barney Sedran

Walter Meanwell

148

TEN AMAZING HALL OF FAMERS

Everyone knows about old-time Basketball Hall of Fame inductees such as George Mikan and Bob Cousy. Here are ten people who were legends in their time and you probably haven't heard of any of them.

1. **Oswald Tower** — This is a man who played his first game of basketball in 1898 and served as an anchor of the rules committee from 1910 to 1959, an amazing 49-year stretch during which basketball went from the inflatable bladder to 15,000 inflated NCAA fans in Louisville's Freedom Hall.

2. **Walter Meanwell** — Walter, who was born in England, at least had a great name for the game. He became a coach in 1911 at Wisconsin, where he developed a system that included short passes, the dribble, pivot plays, and short shots, that radically changed college basketball.

3. **Henry V. Porter** — Along with Oswald Tower, he helped codify basketball rules from coast to coast so at least everyone was playing the same game. As a leader in the National High School Federation, he pioneered the invention of the "molded" basketball, the fan-shaped backboard and the 29½-inch-circumference ball.

4. **Bernhard Borgmann** — This is a man who played in 2,500 professional games, a figure Kareen Abdul-Jabbar might reach if he plays until he's 52. The 5-foot 8-inch Borgmann, who must have never been too far from a suitcase, was an all-league performer in the American, National, Metropolitan, Eastern, New York State and Western Massachusetts leagues.

5. **Barney Sedran** — The 5-foot 4-inch Sedran was the Spud Webb of his day, leading City College of New York in scoring from 1909 to 1911 and playing on 10 championship professional teams after that. In 1913 he scored goals from 25 to 30 feet, shooting at baskets without backboards.

6. **John D. Russell** — Nicknamed "Honey," Russell was a man who made Bernhard Borgmann look lazy by playing in 3,200 professional games over a 28-year career that began while he was in high school. He became the first coach of the Boston Celtics in 1947 and coached Seton Hall to the 1953 NIT title.

7. **Clair Bee** — A man for all reasons, Bee was one of the early giants of college coaching. His Long Island University teams won 95 percent of their games between 1931 and 1951, including the 1939 and 1941 NIT championships. He pioneered the 1-3-1 defense, was primarily responsible for the three-second rule and helped develop the 24-second shot clock. He also wrote the "Chip Hilton" sports books.

8. **Bertha F. Teague** — Bertha coached at Ada Byng (Oklahoma) High School from 1927 until 1969, winning 1,152 games, the national record, and losing 115. Eighteen of her teams won 30 or more games and she went to 22 state championships, winning eight of them.

Clair Bee

Bertha F. Teague

9. **Matthew P. Kennedy** — "Pat" Kennedy became famous as a referee even before the days of the Lite beer commercials. He was a high school, college and professional referee from 1928 to 1946, often working 10 games a week. He was NBA refereeing supervisor from 1946 to 1950, and toured with the Globetrotters from 1950 to 1957.

10. **Charles H. Taylor** — A must on this list, Taylor was twice an Indiana all-state player while at Columbus High School and played 11 years as a professional. But his enduring claim to fame is that in 1931 he began designing the Converse Chuck Taylor basketball shoe, the name that has come to mean "Chucks" to millions of basketball players ever since.

Charles H. Taylor

Matthew P. Kennedy

AMAZING HALL OF FAME QUIZ

Try to match these Basketball Hall of Fame members with their accomplishments:

1. Henry Carlson   *8* A. Led the nation in field goal percent for St. Louis University; played in 7 NBA All-Star games for St. Louis and Boston.

2. Andy Phillip   *7* B. Was the first coach to guide a team in 1000 games at the same college (Western Kentucky University).

3. Henry Iba   *10* C. Led his team to the San Juan title.

4. Paul Endacott   *6* D. Starred for Murray State College before becoming the first superstar of the BAA and NBA in the 1940s.

5. Branch McCracken   *9* E. Averaged 21 points and almost 19 rebounds per game as a LaSalle University All-American in the 1950s.

6. Joseph Fulks   *3* F. Coached Oklahoma State (then A&M) to NCAA titles in 1945 and 1946.

7. Edgar Diddle   *1* G. Coach of University of Pittsburgh, national champions in 1928 and 1930.

8. Edward Macauley   *4* H. Led the University of Kansas to the mythical national title in 1923 and was named Player-of-the-Year.

9. Tom Gola   *2* I. One of the nation's great players at the University of Illinois in the early 1940s; a vital member of the "Whiz Kids."

10. Teddy Roosevelt   *5* J. Led Indiana University in scoring 3 years; then coached the Hoosiers to the 1940 and 1953 NCAA championships.

Complete the following statements:

11. UCLA great John Wooden is the only man inducted into the Hall of Fame as both a player and a coach. Although a legend, Wooden did have one losing season as a basketball coach. That season occurred while Wooden was coaching at   (A) Martinsville, Ind.   (B) UCLA   (C) Purdue   (D) Dayton, Ky.   (E) Marion, Ind.

12. Oklahoma A&M won two national championships with a future Hall of Famer named Bob Kurland at center. Kurland's nickname was (A) Stretch   (B) Bones   (C) Foothills   (D) Big   (E) Crusty.

13. Richard F. D. Barry III often played basketball as plain ol' Rick Barry. He became famous for
(A) scoring 68 points in a playoff game
(B) winning the NBA scoring title three straight years
(C) shooting free throws underhanded
(D) his two-hand set shot
(E) making Bill Russell laugh with his jokes.

14. Although long forgotten,John ''Becky'' Beckman was the greatest draw in professional basketball in the 1920s, when he was known as the ''Babe Ruth of Basketball.'' He was so good in 1927 his team sold him to the Baltimore Orioles basketball team for the then-amazing figure of (A) $500   (B) $50,000   (C) $10,000   (D) $2,465.78   (E) $7,500.

15. Only one Hall of Fame coach has won 100 games at three different colleges: 103 at St. John's, 164 at North Carolina and 283 at South Carolina. That coach is   (A) Babe McCarthy   (B) Bill Foster   (C) Frank McGuire   (D) the other Bill Foster   (E) Billy Donavan.

Chapter 19
PRACTICE MAKES PERFECT (SOMETIMES)
The story of amazing coaches

This Kansas team, which won the mythical national championship in 1923, included the men who would become the two winningest coaches in college basketball history. Adolph Rupp (left, back row) tops the list with 875 wins and Phog Allen (then Kansas coach, second from left, middle row) is second with 771 victories. Dr. Naismith (in the middle) served as an advisor to Allen.

The most telling thing to remember about basketball is that James Naismith, the guy who invented the game, spent very little time coaching it. He knew better. The Doc rarely raised his voice while watching a game and he didn't want to press his luck by moving to the bench.

Naismith, you may recall, never believed his game needed coaches. He didn't even like the concept of a full-time coach. He hadn't invented basketball to give 15,000 students and alumni something to do on a January night. He invented it as a form of physical activity to build bodies and character for the 18 men on the floor. The rules had been written for all to read, so why should the game ever need coaches?

"Basketball is not a game intended merely for amusement," he once wrote, "but it is the attempted solution of a problem."

The Doc's line of thinking was the reason the Intercollegiate Basket Ball Rules Committee authored the 1910 rule that went, "There shall be no coaching during the progress of the game by anybody connected with either of the teams.

"For the violation of this the offending side shall be warned once by the referee, and if the offense is repeated the offended side shall be given a free throw for the basket."

There are a lot of people who wish that rule would have stuck. But it didn't. So now grown men and women coast-to-coast wake up at 4 a.m. worried about the motor skills and academic indifference of elongated high school seniors. That's why good men who lose get the gate and bad men who win are often rewarded with a whole house.

Being a high school coach is an especially tough business. Ninety-nine percent of the time a coach is going to lose the last game of the season and then have to live with that loss for the next eight months, if not 80 years.

The fans, of course, never forget. Suddenly coaches wake up in the morning to find "For Sale" signs in the front yard, and they hadn't even been in contact with a realtor. Angry parents are calling school board members at 3 a.m., and the board members are taking notes. The coach's wife learns it's better to go grocery shopping at 4 a.m., and in another state.

Phillip Hoose, in his book "Hoosiers," describes one Indiana high school coach who had signed a one-year contract with 14 or 15 goals written into it, including winning 10 games.

The coach went 9-11 during the season, but won several more games while capturing the sectional, the first time the school had won the sectional in

30 years. It didn't matter. The coach was asked to resign. He hadn't won 10 games during the regular season.

Coaching in college is even worse because of the money and people involved. The jobs of several assistant coaches, the trainer, the office secretary and even the locker-room manager can be on the line if a head coach starts reading "For Sale" signs on his bluegrass lawn.

And if you do climb to the very top of the profession and earn one of the 23 jobs available with the National Basketball Association, there's a very good chance you'll still be one of the lowest-paid people in your locker room, and with less job security.

What chance does a $200,000-a-year coach with a shaky two-year contract have with a room full of outsized men earning $800,000 a year and their employment guaranteed until 2004?

It all makes one yearn for the wit, wisdom and independence of Arnold "Red" Auerbach, the Boston Celtics legend who in his first year on the job bypassed local Holy Cross whiz Bob Cousy in the first round of the NBA draft for 6-foot-11 Charlie Share of Bowling Green.

The Celtics eventually got Cousy anyway, but how many coaches have longed to stand up before a press conference and say, as Auerbach did, "I didn't give a damn for sentiment or names. That goes for Cousy and everybody else . . . I'm not interested in drafting someone just because he happens to be a local yokel and the fans want him."

A few years later Auerbach won eight consecutive NBA titles.

But 50 years from now, chances are sports fans will have to strain to remember even Arnold Auerbach. The great names of any sport fade away after a few decades — especially in basketball, which still doesn't evoke the "Ruthian" nostalgia of baseball.

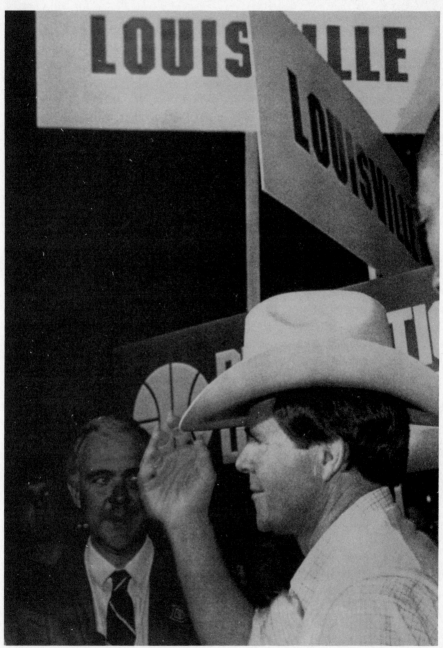

Denny Crum of Louisville, one of today's top coaches, tips his cowboy hat as he arrives in Dallas in 1986. His Cardinals captured their second NCAA championship four days later.

Here, for instance, are:

FIVE AMAZING BUT MOSTLY FORGOTTEN COACHES

1. **Robert L. Douglas** — Douglas was born in the West Indies and came to the United States when he was four. In 1922 he helped organize the all-black Renaissance Five in New York and took them on the road for 22 years in an era when blacks faced horrible discrimination. The Rens won 2,318 games, including 88 in a row in 1933, facing all comers in towns from Boston to Evansville, Indiana.

2. **Everett N. Case** — Case coached for 21 years at four Indiana high schools and won 467 games and four state championships. While most men would have retired after that, Case went to North Carolina State in 1946 and coached another 19 years, winning at least 20 games a year from 1947 to 1956. His 40-year record was 844 wins, 258 losses.

3. **Howard Hobson** — Coach of the University of Oregon team that won the first NCAA tournament in 1939, Hobson also became famous while coaching at Yale by pioneering intersectional play between the two coasts. The cost of college basketball has never been the same.

4. **Joe Lapchick** — Because of financial pressure from home, Lapchick turned to playing professional basketball before finishing high school. He played for 19 years, from 1917-1936, including five years with the famed Original Celtics. He then coached at St. John's University for 20 years, winning four NIT championships, and coached the New York Knicks for eight years.

5. **Everett Shelton** — Shelton coached the 1937 Denver Safeways to the AAU national championship. In 1943 he won the NCAA title while coaching at the University of Wyoming. He won 850 games over an amazingly varied 46-year career.

THE AMAZING LIST OF THE TOP TEN ALL-TIME WINNINGEST COLLEGE COACHES

	Coach	Wins	School(s)
1.	Adolph Rupp	875	Kentucky
2.	Phog Allen	771	Kansas, Baker, Haskell, Central Missouri State
3.	Clarence "Big House" Gaines	769	Winston-Salem
4.	Henry Iba	767	Northwest Missouri, Colorado, Oklahoma State
5.	Ed Diddle	759	Western Kentucky
6.	Ray Meyer	724	DePaul
7.	John Wooden	667	Indiana State, UCLA
8.	Bloomer Sullivan	662	Southeastern Oklahoma
9.	Ed Adams	645	North Carolina Central, Tuskegee, Texas Southern
10.	John Lance	643	Southwest Oklahoma, Pittsburgh State (Kansas)

THE AMAZING LIST OF THE TOP TEN ALL-TIME WINNINGEST NBA COACHES

	Coach	Won	Lost	Percentage
1.	Red Auerbach	938	479	.662
2.	Jack Ramsay	826	732	.530
3.	Dick Motta	808	750	.519
4.	Gene Shue	757	768	.496
5.	Bill Fitch	716	678	.514
6.	Red Holzman	696	604	.535
7.	Cotton Fitzsimmons	588	634	.481
8.	Lenny Wilkens	584	542	.519
9.	John MacLeod	579	543	.516
10.	Al Attles	557	518	.518

Clarence "Big House" Gaines, who was born in Paducah, Kentucky, is the winningest active college coach.

Controversial Indiana coach Bob Knight led his Hoosiers to the 1987 NCAA title in New Orleans. He leads active Division I coaches with three championships.

THE AMAZING COACHES' QUOTES QUIZ

Try to match the coach on the left with his quote on the right.

1. Phog Allen — 4 A. On women: "There's only two things you people are good for: having kids and frying bacon."

2. Red Auerbach — 9 B. "I'm not out to conquer the world, just to win all the basketball games my team plays."

3. Nat Holman — 6 C. Defining a pressure game: "It's when you look at a cheerleader and don't notice her body."

4. Bob Knight — 5 D. "When I made the varsity at Boys High, I needed $1.25 for an athletic supporter. My dad thought that was a lot to spend on such a small investment."

5. Frank Layden — 3 E. "It's not what you can do with a ball that counts, it's knowing what to do without a ball that's important."

6. Al McGuire — 2 F. "There's only one dynasty, baby! And that's right here."

7. George Raveling — 1 G. "You're not old until it takes you longer to rest up than it does to get tired."

8. Lee Rose — 10 H. "Be quick, but never hurry."

9. Adolph Rupp — 8 I. "I would like to deny the statement that I think basketball is a matter of life and death. I feel it's much more important than that."

10. John Wooden — 7 J. "The best three years of a sportswriter's life are the third grade."

Chapter 20
HOW'S YOUR BLINDFOLDED
FREE THROW SHOOTING?
Amazing streaks and records

The amazing Allen Brothers (including Phog Allen who became the legendary coach at Kansas) set new standards for family basketball, as well as ugly knees. They defeated many of the best amateur teams of their era. The Allen Brothers Basketball Team, from the left, Harry B. "Pete," Forrest C. "Phog," Homer P. Sr., Elmer M., Hubert L., and Richard C.; in front, Homer P., Jr. Circa, early 1900s.

Technically speaking, the term "free throw" is left over from the early days when a basketball wasn't "shot" at the basket, it was "thrown" at the basket, and not always very well. The free throw is the shot that's won or lost 100,000 basketball games, but has never gotten full respect. Maybe this list will help (although we doubt it).

(1) Ted St. Martin, a man who made his living traveling around the country shooting free throws, once hit 2,036 consecutive free throws, a record that should stand until some other great shooter has three days with nothing else to do.

(2) The all-time record for most consecutive underhand free throws by a guy with an animal's name belongs to Harold "Bunny" Levitt, who on April 6, 1935, canned 499 consecutive free throws underhanded, missed one, then hit another 371 in a row. Since no one has shot a free throw underhand in almost 15 years, his record might last longer than St. Martin's.

(3) For sheer grace under pressure, however, neither St. Martin or Levitt can hold a backboard to the immortal Wilfred Hetzel.

Hetzel, the story goes, began his trick-shot career firing underhand shots at a barrel hoop nailed to a woodshed at his home at Melrose, Minnesota. Since he didn't always have a basketball, he would sometimes use a football, wadded-up rags, and maybe even his kid sister.

He never did become good enough to make the team at Melrose, but he continued to shoot, and eventually became nationally-famous for his ability to make shots from 15, 30 and even 70 feet. According to the *All-Sports Record Book* from the 1930s, Hetzel set these never-to-be broken free-throw records in various exhibitions:

Standing on left foot only, 53 straight.
Standing on right foot only, 38 straight.
Both feet on floor, left eye closed, 42 straight.
Both feet on floor, right eye closed, 18 straight.
One-handed shots standing on left foot, 15 straight.
One-handed shots standing on right foot, 11 straight.
You just don't see exhibitions like that anymore.

(4) Bill Harvey of Hampton Bays, New York, and Rusty Marshall of Roberts, Montana, each made 38 free throws in a high school game, which is the national record. Second place is held by Randy Patti of Kansas City Rosedale who hit 31 of 32 shots, including the last 31 in a row.

(5) The all-time career high school free-throw percentage shooter is (who else?) Steve Alford of New Castle, Indiana, who hit 546 of 616 for 88.6 percent. The one-season record was set by Daryl Moreau of New Orleans de LaSalle who hit 119 of 122 in 1978-79 for a 97.5 percent average.

(6) Proving the free-throw shooting style of Bunny Levitt and Wilfred Hetzel to be the best ever invented, Rick Barry is the all-time best NBA shooter with an even .900 percentage on 3,818 out of 4,243 chances. Calvin Murphy (3,445 of 3,864) is second at .892.

(7) The NBA record for most free throws made in a game is 28 set by Adrian Dantley and, amazingly enough, Wilt Chamberlain. Wilt's 32 attempts in his 100 point game is also the NBA record.

(8) Oscar Robertson made 7,694 free throws in his NBA career, the league record. Jerry West is second with 7,160. Wilt Chamberlain took 11,862 free throws in his career, but hit only 6,057 for a lifetime .511 percent.

(9) Craig Collins of Penn State holds the Division I NCAA free throw record for a season; he made 94 of 98 in 1985 for a 95.9 percent. Harvard ranks first (1984) at 82.2 percent and second (1985) at 81.1 percent on the list of team leaders. This probably means they didn't have cheerleaders to distract them.

(10) Pete Maravich hit 30 of 31 free throws in a 1969 game against Oregon State, a major-college record for most free throws in one game that still stands.

(11) John T. Sebastian made 63 consecutive free throws while blindfolded at Maine Township East High School on May 18, 1972. Fred L. Newman of San Jose, California, made 88 consecutive free throws while blindfolded at the Central YMCA, San Jose, California on February 5, 1978.

TEN TRULY AMAZING RECORDS THAT
WILL NEVER BE BROKEN

1. CCNY defeated Rensselaer Poly in 1911, 20-5, and missed 15 of 15 free throws.
2. William Miller scored all of Michigan's points (14) in 1921 against Indiana.
3. In an AAU game at Pacific Lutheran University on January 16, 1970, Steve Myers sank a shot while standing out of bounds at the other end of the court. Though the basket was illegal, the officials give in to crowd sentiment and allowed the points to count. The distance was claimed to be 92 feet 3½ inches from measurements made 10 years later.
4. In 1930, L. E. Leevy of League (Texas) High School made 143 consecutive field goals.

Steve Alford

5. Loudon (Tenn.) High School tallied 94 points in the fourth quarter vs. Athens McMinn County in 1956.

6. In 1984, Cindy Harms of Allison Bristow High School (Iowa) scored all of her team's points in a 67-54 triumph over Grundy Center.

7. Two West Virginia boys' high school teams were whistled for a total of 110 personal fouls in a 1954 game. Weston (59 fouls) and Grafton (51) probably didn't go out for malts together after the game.

8. DeQuincy Grand Avenue High School (La.) mercifully held the score to 211-29 in a 1964 victory over Cameron Audery Memorial.

9. In 1969, Chattanooga East Ridge High School (Tenn.) outlasted Voltewah, 38-37, in 16 overtimes.

10. Walter Garrett of Birmingham West End (Alabama) High School scored all of his team's points in a 97-54 romp over Birmingham Glenn Vocational in 1963. It was his final game and his teammates fed him the ball constantly and either deliberately missed when they shot or didn't shoot at all. In the closing minutes, to prevent Garrett from hitting 100, all five of the Glenn Vocational players guarded him.

THE AMAZING RECORDS AND STREAKS QUIZ

1. Who is the only player to lead the NCAA (Division I) in scoring and rebounding in the same year?

2. Which SEC team didn't make its first appearance in the NCAA tournament until 1987?

3. Wilt Chamberlain and _____ are the only players in NBA history to score more than 3000 points in one season.

4. The major-college record for the most wins in a season (since 1938) is held by _____ with 37:
   A. Georgetown, 1985
   B. Indiana, 1987
   C. UCLA, 1973
   D. Kentucky, 1948
   E. Duke, 1986

5. This player is second on the college Division I list of scoring averages for his career at 34.6 points per game from 1969-71:
   A. Oscar Robertson
   B. Austin Carr
   C. Elvin Hayes
   D. Rick Mount
   E. Rick Barry

Rick Barry, the all-time best NBA free throw shooter is shown in 1972 as a member of the ABA New York Nets.

166

6. This player leads college players in career field-goal percentage with 67.8:
   A. Bill Walton
   B. Lew Alcindor
   C. Steve Johnson
   D. Jerry Lucas
   E. Henry Finkel

7. This player is the NCAA leader in career free-throw percentage at 90.9 percent:
   A. Steve Alford
   B. Rod Foster
   C. Bill Bradley
   D. Greg Starrick
   E. Lee Bukstel

8. This player is the NCAA career leader in rebounds per game at 22.7:
   A. Bill Russell
   B. Wilt Chamberlain
   C. Artis Gilmore
   D. Tom Gola
   E. George Mikan

9. Only three college players have averaged more than 40 points per game in a season. Pete Maravich accomplished this feat three years in a row. The other two are:
   A. Austin Carr and Bill Walton
   B. Frank Selvy and Johnny Neumann
   C. Elvin Hayes and Billy McGill
   D. Wilt Chamberlain and Freeman Williams
   E. Oscar Robertson and Jerry West

10. Name the five NBA players who have won three or more Most Valuable Player awards.

11. Until Wilt Chamberlain broke his mark five times in 1961 and 1962, _____ held the single-game NBA scoring record with 71 points (set November 15, 1960.)

12. On January 19, 1974, _____ ended UCLA's record 88-game winning streak, 71-70, by rallying from an 11-point deficit in the last 3 minutes, 32 seconds.

13. On January 9, 1972, Kareem Abdul-Jabbar and his Milwaukee Bucks stopped the longest winning streak in the modern history of pro team sports by defeating the _____, who had won 33 in a row.

14. The NBA record for playing in the most consecutive games is 906, held by _____:
    A. John Havlicek
    B. John Kerr
    C. Jerry West
    D. Kareem Abdul-Jabbar
    E. Randy Smith
15. In 1951, the Harlem Globetrotters set an all-time attendance record by playing before 75,000 in _____:
    A. Chicago
    B. Montreal
    C. New York
    D. Simpsonville, Kentucky
    E. West Berlin, Germany

THE AMAZING NBA LEADERS QUIZ

Match the catagory on the left with the top three all-time career leaders in that catagory on the right (through the 1986-87 season).

1. Points   A. Gus Williams, Maurice Cheeks, Julius Erving

2. Rebounds   B. Kareem Abdul-Jabbar, Elvin Hayes, John Havlicek

3. Assists   C. Kareem Abdul-Jabbar, Elvin Hayes, Hal Greer

4. Free Throws Made   D. Kareem Abdul-Jabbar, Wilt Chamberlain, Elvin Hayes

5. Blocked Shots   E. Kareem Abdul-Jabbar, Wayne Rollins, George T. Johnson

6. Steals   F. Oscar Robertson, Lenny Wilkens, Bob Cousy

7. Disqualifications on Fouls   G. Oscar Robertson, Jerry West, Dolph Schayes

8. Games Played   H. Vern Mikkelsen, Walter Dukes, Charlie Share

9. Free Throws Attempted   I. Wilt Chamberlain, Bill Russell, Kareem Abdul-Jabbar

10. Personal Fouls   J. Wilt Chamberlain, Oscar Robertson, Kareem Abdul-Jabbar

Kareem Abdul-Jabbar, who was then known as Lew Alcindor, is shown during a high school workout in 1965. He is now the all-time leader in seven of the 13 major NBA statistical categories.

OTHER AMAZING RECORDS AND STREAKS

1. Each of these seven stars averaged at least 20 points and 20 rebounds per game for his major-college career:
   A. Walt Dukes, Seton Hall, 1952-53
   B. Bill Russell, San Francisco, 1954-56
   C. Elgin Baylor, College of Idaho and Seattle, 1955, 1957-58
   D. Paul Silas, Creighton, 1962-64
   E. Julius Erving, Massachusetts, 1970-71
   F. Artis Gilmore, Jacksonville, 1970-71
   G. Kermit Washington, American, 1971-73
2. Bill Chambers of William and Mary holds the NCAA (Division I) record for most rebounds in a game with 51 against Virginia in 1953.
3. UCLA defeated the University of California 52 straight times over a 25-year period, before the streak was broken in 1986.
4. In 1907 the immortal G. Kinney of Yale took the seven-team Eastern Intercollegiate League scoring title with a whopping 31 points on the year. Pete Maravich could score that many in a single game before his socks started to droop.
5. The Military Nice Guy Award with a wimp-leaf cluster goes to the 1918-1919 Virginia Polytechnic Institute teams, which didn't foul out a single player over the two seasons.
6. The all-time record for number of players in a basketball game was set in the early 1890s when Ed Hitchcock Jr., a Cornell College instructor, introduced basketball to an amazing 100 students at the same time. This cattle call came to a merciful end when school administrators, worried that a rush of 100 players from one end of the floor to the other would literally bring down the gymnasium, told Hitchcock to slim down the sides a little. By 1895 most men's games were being played five to a side.
7. There were 781 teams entered in the 1934-35 Indiana high school basketball tournament, meaning that 780 games had to be played over three consecutive weekends to pick a winner.
8. UCLA won 38 straight games in NCAA tournament play, a streak that included seven straight national championships, 1967-73.

THE AMAZING NBA LEADERS QUIZ ANSWERS

1. D	6. A
2. I	7. H
3. F	8. B
4. G	9. J
5. E	10. C

THE AMAZING RECORDS AND STREAKS QUIZ ANSWERS

1. Xavier McDaniel of Wichita State, who averaged 27.2 points and 14.8 rebounds in 1985.
2. The Florida Gators, who lost to the eventual runner-up Syracuse Orangemen.
3. Chicago's Michael Jordan with 3041 points, for a 37.1 average. Wilt had more than 3000 points 3 times; he set the record with 4029 (50.4 average) in the 1961-62 season.
4. E. Duke, 1986. The Blue Devils lost to Louisville in the championship game of the NCAA tournament. Second is Kentucky, 1948, with 36 victories.
5. B. Austin Carr, Notre Dame.
6. C. Steve Johnson, Oregon State.
7. D. Greg Starrick, Kentucky and Southern Illinois.
8. C. Artis Gilmore, Jacksonville.
9. B. Frank Selvy and Johnny Neumann.
10. Kareem Abdul-Jabbar, Milwaukee-L.A. Lakers (6) — 1971, 72, 74, 76, 77, 80.
    Bill Russell, Boston (5) — 1958, 61, 62, 63, 65.
    Wilt Chamberlain, Philadelphia (4) — 1960, 66, 67, 68.
    Moses Malone, Houston and Philadelphia (3) — 1979, 82, 83.
    Larry Bird, Boston (3) — 1984, 85, 86.
11. Elgin Baylor.
12. Notre Dame.
13. Los Angeles Lakers.
14. E. Randy Smith (Buffalo, San Diego, Cleveland, New York, San Diego) from February 18, 1972 through March 13, 1983.
15. E. West Berlin, Germany.

Chapter 21
"THE RIFLEMAN," RED SQUARE
AND "BASKETBALL TECHNIQUES
SET TO MUSIC"
Amazing trivia

AN AMAZING LIST OF SIGNIFICANT BASKETBALL BOOKS AND ARTICLES PUBLISHED FROM 1891 TO 1947

(from "Annotated Bibliography of Basketball Literature" by Robert M. Bruce — published by the National Association of Basketball Coaches)

1. Allen, J. P., "Basketball, the Athletic Fad this Year," *Scholastic Coach,* March, 1934.

2. Carlson, M. C., "Tonic and Phasic Actions of the Muscles in Basket Shooting," *Athletic Journal,* December, 1934.

3. Cook, M. B., "A Basketball Meet by Mail," *Athletic Journal,* May, 1942.

4. Frost, H., and Wardlaw, C. D.,*Basketball and Indoor Baseball for Women.* New York: Charles Scribner's Sons, 1920, 154 pp.

5. Garveer, H., "Are Basketball Tournaments Harmful?" *Hygeia,* March 1929.

6. Leavitt, H.,"How to Throw 499 Fouls," *Scholastic Coach,* February, 1936.

7. Lersch, G., "Crow's Nest Basketball Officiating," *Official Basketball Guide,* 1943-44.

8. Nerenberg, J., "Golf Basketball" *Journal of Health and Physical Education,* February, 1939.

9. Owen, W. B., "Are Basketball Coaches 'Dumbbells'?" *Scholastic Coach,* November, 1938.

10. Wakerfield, M. C., "A Study of Mortality among the Men Who Have Played in the Indiana State Final Basketball Tournaments," *Research Quarterly,* 15:2-11, March, 1944.

11. Whitaker, T. G., "Water Basketball — New Aquatic Game," *Mind and Body,* p. 37, March, 1914.

12. Yanisch, D. I., "Basketball Techniques Set to Music," *Journal of Health and Physical Education,* 17:299, May, 1946.

The tallest player of all time is reputed to be Suleiman Ali Nashnush (born 1943) who played for the Libyan team in 1962, measuring 8 feet tall.

Opposite page: Chuck Connors stars in 1974 as the famed Apache leader, Geronimo.

THE AMAZING JACK-OF-ALL-TRADES QUIZ

Match these talented athletes with their basketball accomplishments.

A. Hank Greenberg (Baseball
Hall of Fame)

B. Chuck Connors (Starred on
the TV series, "The
Rifleman"; played in 1951
for the Chicago Cubs)

C. Otto Graham (Football
Hall of Fame)

D. Mike Warren (TV shows
include "The White Shadow"
and "Hill Street Blues")

E. Lou Boudreau (Baseball
Hall of Fame)

F. Curt Gowdy (Award-winning
sportscaster)

G. Jackie Robinson (Baseball
Hall of Fame)

H. Bud Grant (Longtime coach of
the NFL Minnesota Vikings)

I. Dick Groat (Pittsburgh Pirate,
MVP of the National League
in 1960)

1. Talented member of basketball
team at Northwestern

2. All-conference basketball
guard at Wyoming in the
1940s

3. Basketball All-American at
Duke

4. Member of 1949-50 NBA
champion Minneapolis Lakers

5. Starred in basketball for NYU

6. Led Pacific Coast Conference
in scoring in 1940 for UCLA

7. Basketball starter at UCLA
during Lew Alcindor era

8. Member of Boston Celtics
in the late 1940s

9. Pro basketball player in
1939-40

How far does a basketball player run during a game? Of course, the distance can vary greatly, but some years ago, Ben Peck, coach at Middlebury, Vermont, decided to find out. He put pedometers on the feet of his players.

The results: Overall, his team traveled a total of 24.01 miles, 11.97 in the first half and 12.04 in the second half. Forward Fred Lapham ran the farthest, 5.31 miles. The other forward, Tom Neidhart, covered 5.14 miles. Center Bob Adsit ran 4.25 miles. The guards averaged 2.66 miles each.

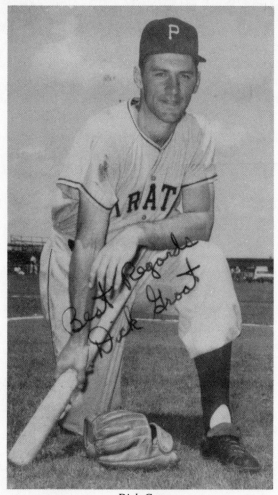

Dick Groat

Otto Graham

On February 21, 1953, at Albany, New York, Niagara and Siena played the first six-overtime-period game, with Niagara finally winning 88-81 after three hours and two minutes of play.

As regulation time ran out, Niagara's Gerry Kennedy tossed in a long one-hander that would have won the game. But the officials didn't hear the buzzer. The Siena timer claimed that time had expired and the Niagara representative disagreed. After a ten-minute discussion the officials ruled no basket.

Eddie Fleming of Niagara played the full seventy minutes, and his jersey number thereafter was changed to seventy in recognition of this feat.

NIAGARA	25	29	7	2	7	2	4	12 — 88
SIENA	24	30	7	2	7	2	4	5 — 81

The longest measured field goal in a college game was 89 feet 3 inches by Les Henson of Virginia Tech, on January 21, 1980. Henson, a left-handed shooter, heaved the ball almost the full length of the court with his right hand just as the final buzzer sounded to give Virginia Tech a 79-77 victory over Florida State. The NCAA does not officially recognize a record for the longest shot — there is no standard for measuring — but it did report that the measurement was made from Henson's back foot to the back of the rim (which is 6 inches from the backboard).

Andy Landers, coach of the women's team at Georgia, made his players wear unwashed uniforms for a week because he thought the team's defense was stinky.

THESE WERE THE PLAYERS ON
THE WORST TEAM IN NBA HISTORY,
THE 1972-73 PHILADELPHIA 76ers
(9 WINS - 73 LOSSES)

Player	Games	Scoring Average
Fred Carter	81	20.0
John Block	48	17.9
Tom Van Arsdale	30	17.7
Bill Bridges	10	14.0
Kevin Loughery	32	13.9
Leroy Ellis	69	13.7
Manny Leaks	82	11.0
Fred Boyd	82	10.5
John Q. Trapp	39	10.7
Don May	39	11.9
Jeff Halliburton	31	11.9
Hal Greer	38	9.5
Dale Schlueter	78	5.6
Dave Sorenson	48	5.9
Dennis Awtrey	3	2.3
Mel Counts	7	1.4
Luther Green	5	0.6
Bob Rule	3	0.0

AMAZINGLY UNSUCCESSFUL TEAMS IN THE
NCAA TOURNAMENT
(ALL-TIME RECORDS)

North Carolina A & T	0-6	Furman	1-7
Eastern Kentucky	0-5	Tulsa	1-6
Marshall	0-5	Bowling Green	1-5
Yale	0-4	Middle Tennessee State	1-5
Rhode Island	0-3	Old Dominion	1-4
Iona	0-3	Toledo	1-4
Loyola (La.)	0-3	Miami (Oh.)	3-14
San Diego St.	0-3	Connecticut	4-14
Southern U.	0-3		

How many NBA championship teams did Red Auerbach coach that didn't include Bill Russell?

Answer: Zero

The American Basketball League Standings — 1934-35

FIRST HALF	W	L	PC	SECOND HALF	W	L	PC
New York Jewels	16	6	.727	Philadelphia Hebrews	12	7	.632
Philadelphia Hebrews	13	10	.565	Brooklyn Visitations	12	7	.632
Brooklyn Visitations	13	11	.542	New Britain**	9	9	.500
Newark Mules	12	11	.522	Jersey Reds	9	9	.500
Boston Trojans	10	11	.476	New York Jewels	8	10	.444
Jersey Reds	7	14	.318	Boston Trojans	4	12	.250
New Britain	6	14	.300	**Starting second half New Britain and Newark consolidated.			

The Brooklyn Visitations won the league championship by first defeating the Philadelphia Hebrews 2 games to 1, then beating the New York Jewels 3 to 2.

THE AMAZING BASKETBALL
QUIZ YOU CAN'T LOSE

Match the nickname on the left with player on the right.

1. Red
2. Red
3. Red
4. Red
5. Red
6. Red
7. Red
8. Red

A. Auerbach
B. Holtzman
C. Kerr
D. Koltz
E. Murrell
F. Robbins
G. Square
H. Sea

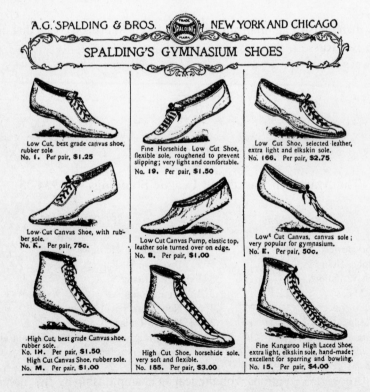

From an early Spalding catalog.

Wilt Chamberlain had more influence on the rules of basketball than any other individual in the history of the game. Wilt was legislated against three times during his college career, even though he played only two years.

Wilt's technique of taking a run and dunking his free throws was banned by one rule, his scoring was diminished by the offensive goal-tending rule, and the inbounds pass over the backboard was outlawed because of Wilt.

Just how rough was this early game of basketball? It was so rough that it often was the duty of the team captain to leave a window open in the dressing room so the players, and the officials, could make a safe departure in the event the locals took exception to the evening's proceedings.

In 1929 Frank Andresko, one of the players in a basketball game played at Oshkosh, Wisconsin, was thrown against the wall and had his jersey torn when the basketball suddenly exploded.

The immortal Scot DuVal, a Chicago commodities trader, whipped Magic Johnson 13-8 in the Southern Comfort National Nerf Ball Championships of 1987 at the Red Onion lounge in Beverly Hills. DuVal won with a turn-around jump shot as Johnson blew a junior skyhook.

Rabum County High School beat Towns County in Clayton, Georgia, 129-41, but only because Towns County, mad at the officials, scored 56 points in the Rabum basket.

Television revenue from the Division I men's NCAA basketball tournament has become so important that in 1986-87 it supplied an amazing 76.4 percent of the association's $57.4 million budget. Football supplied 2.4 percent.

For some reason, Hollywood has made as many great movies about basketball, or even with basketball in the background, as it has about dwarf mud wrestling. Here's a list of some of the more memorable basketball films:

1. "The Harlem Globetrotters" (1951) — The famed team stars and has a few romantic encounters.

2. "Go Man, Go" (1954) — The formation of the Harlem Globetrotters and their rise to fame, starring Sidney Poitier and Dane Clark.

3. "Drive, He Said" (1972) — Youth alienation on a college campus, starring Karen Black, Jack Nicholson and Bruce Dern.

4. "Maurie" (1973) — The life of Maurice Stokes, a paralyzed basketball player, and his friend, Jack Twyman.

5. "Mixed Company" (1974) — A basketball coach's wife insists on adopting a black, an Oriental and an Indian. Starring Joseph Bologna.

6. "The Fish That Saved Pittsburgh" (1979) — A losing basketball team experiments with astrology. Cast includes Julius Erving, Stockard Channing, Jonathan Winters, Meadowlark Lemon, Flip Wilson and Kareem Abdul-Jabbar.

7. "Fast Break" (1979) — A basketball coach (Gabe Kaplan) brings his New York street players with him to a midwestern college. Cast includes Mike Warren and Bernard King.

8. "The Harlem Globetrotters on Gilligan's Island" (1981) — Gilligan and his gang are visited by the Globetrotters, a mad scientist and basketball-playing robots. With Bob Denver, Scatman Crothers and Jim Backus.

9. "Hoosiers" (1986) — A small town in Indiana wins the state basketball championship. Gene Hackman stars in the role of head coach; Dennis Hopper was nominated for an Oscar (best supporting actor) as the alcoholic father of one of the players.

AN AMAZING LIST OF STAR PLAYERS WHO NEVER PLAYED IN THE NCAA TOURNAMENT

1. Ed Macauley, St Louis
2. Walter Dukes, Seton Hall
3. Bailey Howell, Mississippi State
4. Walt Bellamy, Indiana
5. Rick Barry, Miami (Fla.)
6. Pete Maravich, LSU
7. Julius Erving, Massachusetts

Gene Hackman and his players in "Hoosiers."

Bill Cartwright made $25,694.44 per minute for the New York Knicks in the 1985-86 season (36 minutes for $925,000).

Who were the Knickerbockers' centers on that night in 1962 when Wilt Chamberlain scored his record 100 points against New York?

Wilt set the all-time NBA one-game scoring record on March 2, 1962, tossing in an even 100 points, many on tip-ins which now would be illegal because of the NBA's offensive goal-tending rule (which was adopted just a couple of years after Chamberlain's record was set).

The Knicks used four centers that record night; Darrall Imhoff played for 20 minutes and managed but 7 points, while Dave Budd played for 27 minutes and scored 13 points. Johnny Green and Cleveland Buckner also took brief turns against Chamberlain.

AMAZINGLY FREAKISH SCORES

Kansas State 24, Salina 0 in 1905

Kansas State 60, Haskell 0 in 1905

Kansas State 10, Kansas Normal 0 in 1905

Kansas 28, Kansas State 0 in 1905

Pennsylvania 17, Cornell 16 in 1909, with Charles Keinath scoring all 17 points.

Bucknell 159, Philadelphia College of Pharmacy 5 in 1903

AMAZING AWARD FOR THE BEST BASKETBALL NAME

Wagner University center Largest Agbejemisin

AMAZING AWARD FOR THE WORST BASKETBALL NAME

Frank Brickowski of the Seattle Supersonics

In November 1954, George Mikan scored 15 of the losers' points (or 83 percent) as the Fort Wayne Pistons beat the Minneapolis Lakers, 19-18.

ALL BY HIMSELF

Ever hear of a one-man team? Pat McGee of St. Peter's High School in Fairmont, West Virginia, won a basketball game all by himself.

On March 16, 1937, the St. Peter's seniors played an intramural basketball game against the sophomores. With the score tied 32-all, and four minutes and a few seconds left, all of Pat's teammates had fouled out.

Standing alone, Pat McGee not only kept the sophomores from scoring but added three points to his team's total by sinking a basket from the floor and adding a foul shot. Final score: seniors 35, sophomores 32!

One of the screwiest basketball games on record pitted Allegany Community College of Cumberland, Maryland, against Baltimore Prep Institute. The final score read Allegany 210, Baltimore Prep 23. The grotesque tally was attributed, by the losing coach, to someone's tinkering with the clock.

"The clock," said the coach, Alan Raskin, "stayed stopped when we had the ball and it didn't start running until they got it. I told my scorekeeper about it and the timekeeper told him that the button was stuck. I told the officials about it and they said there was nothing they could do about it."

In 1965 All-American forward Wayne Estes was killed in a freak accident after playing the best game of his career. Estes, foremost scorer in Utah State's history, had just led the school to victory over Denver by scoring 48 points. Upon leaving the fieldhouse at Logan, Utah, Estes and three buddies were headed for a restaurant when they witnessed a car accident. The automobile had skidded into a traffic island and spun into a metal utility pole. The pole, which held a high-tension wire, dropped it to about six feet from the ground. In attempting to walk under it, the 6-foot-5 Estes bumped the line with his forehead. He was electrocuted. Had he been three inches shorter, his head wouldn't have hit the wire.

In another horrifying incident, West Texas State University lost one of the best basketball prospects ever enrolled at the school. One night following his return from Thanksgiving vacation, freshman Alton Crook left his dormitory and walked to a gasoline station. He told the attendant his car was stalled and asked for a five-gallon can of fuel. He took the can and disappeared down an alley. A minute later the attendant saw Crook, a mass of flames, staggering toward him, fatally burned, and later a subject of mystery.

The late "Phog" Allen, longtime coach at Kansas, also coached Bess Truman's high school team.

THE AMAZING ALL-HOROSCOPE TEAM
(The best active NBA player born under each sign)

CAPRICORN Dec. 22-Jan. 19 — Dominique Wilkins (born Jan. 12, 1960 Paris, France)

AQUARIUS Jan. 20.-Feb. 18 — Michael Jordan (born Feb. 17, 1963 Brooklyn, N.Y.)

PISCES Feb. 19-March 20 — Charles Barkley (born Feb. 20, 1963 Leeds, Ala.)

ARIES March 21-April 19 — Kareem Abdul-Jabbar (born April 16, 1947 New York, N.Y.)

TAURUS April 20-May 20 — Isiah Thomas (born April 30, 1961 Chicago)

GEMINI May 21-June 20 — Xavier McDaniel (born June 4, 1963 Columbia, S.C.)

CANCER June 21-July 22 — Ralph Sampson (born July 7, 1960 Harrisonburg, Va.)

LEO July 23-Aug. 22 — Earvin "Magic" Johnson (born August 14, 1959 Lansing, Michigan)

VIRGO Aug. 23-Sept. 22 — Sidney Moncrief (Born Sept. 21, 1957 Little Rock, Ark.)

LIBRA Sept. 23-Oct. 22 — Brad Daugherty (born Oct. 19, 1965 Black Mountain, N.C.)

SCORPIO Oct. 23-Nov. 21 — Bill Walton (born Nov. 5, 1952 Mesa, Cal.)

SAGITTARIUS Nov. 22-Dec. 21 — Larry Bird (born Dec. 7, 1956 French Lick, Ind.)

Opposite page: Jeane Dixon, astrologer, who probably never dreamed she would appear in a basketball book.

Match the last names with the nickname. Part 1 is meant for less experienced fans, Part 2 for the experts.

THE AMAZING NICKNAME QUIZ — PART 1

1. Charles "Cotton"
2. "Downtown Freddie"
3. Earl "The Pearl"
4. "Easy Ed"
5. Jim "Bad News"
6. John "Hondo"
7. "Jungle Jim"
8. Nate "Tiny"
9. Robert "Hot Rod"
10. Tom "Satch"

A. Archibald
B. Barnes
C. Brown
D. Havlicek
E. Hundley
F. Loscutoff
G. Macauley
H. Monroe
I. Nash
J. Sanders

THE AMAZING NICKNAME QUIZ — PART 2

11. Art "Hambone"
12. Bill "The Hill"
13. Bill "Secretary of the Defense"
14. Bob "Big Blue"
15. Bob "Butterbean"
16. Chet "The Jet"
17. Dan "Dogpatch"
18. Dave "The Rave"
19. David "Big Daddy"
20. Dean "The Dream"
21. Jerry "Zeke from Cabin Creek"
22. Larry "Special K"
23. Roger "The Rifle"
24. Wade "Swede"
25. Wayne "Baby Huey"
26. William "Pickles"

K. Estes
L. Halbrook
M. Kennedy
N. Kenon
O. Lattin
P. Love
Q. McGill
R. Meminger
S. Pettit
T. Russell
U. Stallworth
V. Strickland
W. Swartz
X. Walker
Y. West
Z. Williams

ALL-OUTDOOR TEAM

Captain Glenn RIVERS, Hawks
Kenny FIELDS, Clippers
Greg KITE, Celtics
Perry MOSS, Warriors
Louis ORR, Knicks
6th man - BROOK Steppe, Kings

These teams have never made the Final Four in college basketball (number of appearances in NCAA tournament):

Alabama (8)
Arizona State (9)
Boston College (8)
BYU (12)
Connecticut (13)
Illinois (11)
Maryland (9)   *FINISHED THIRD TWICE*

Missouri (9)
Navy (8)
Pepperdine (8)
St. Joseph's (Pa.) (13)
Tennessee (8)
Utah State (10)

Honorable mention: Notre Dame with one Final Four trip in 20 appearances.

"Easy Ed"

THE AMAZING ANIMAL NICKNAME QUIZ

Match each of these basketball personalities with the correct nickname.

1. Fred Carter	A. Bunny
2. Everett Case	B. Cat
3. Harry Gallatin	C. Doggy
4. Alvin Julian	D. Goose
5. Ed Krause	E. The Horse
6. Ward Lampert	F. Houndog
7. Harold Levitt	G. Kangaroo Kid
8. Jim Ligon	H. Mad Dog
9. Ted McLain	I. Monk
10. Don Meineke	J. Moose
11. Jim Pollard	K. Old Gray Fox
12. John Thompson	L. Piggy

"Cat"

ALL-OCCUPATION TEAM

Captain Bernard KING, Knicks
Randy BREUER, Bucks
Gary PLUMMER, Warriors
Terry PORTER, Trailblazers
Granville WAITERS, Bulls

ALL-AVIARY TEAM

Captain Larry BIRD, Celtics
Otis BIRDSONG, Nets
Michael CAGE, Clippers
TREE Rollins, Hawks
Rory SPARROW, Knicks

TWENTY AMAZING NICKNAMES FOR COLLEGE TEAMS

1. Albany State (N.Y.) "Great Danes"
2. Benthany (Kans.) "Terrible Swedes"
3. Cal-Irvine "Anteaters"
4. Heidelberg (Ohio) "Student Princes"
5. Huron (S.D.) "Scalpers"
6. Idaho "Vandals"
7. Kansas State-Pittsburg "Gorillas"
8. Lincoln Memorial (Tenn.) "Railsplitters"
9. Marshall (W. Va.) "Thundering Herd"
10. Oglethorpe (Ga.) "Stormy Petrels"
11. Presbyterian (S.C.) "Blue Hose"
12. Pomona-Pitzer (Cal.) "Sagehens"
13. St. Louis (Mo.) "Billikens"
14. Southern Illinois-Carbondale "Salukis"
15. Southwest Louisiana "Ragin' Cajuns"
16. South Dakota Tech. "Hardrockers"
17. Southern State (Ark.) "Muleriders"
18. Thomas Jefferson (Pa.) "Medics"
19. Washburn (Kans.) "Ichabods"
20. Whittier (Cal.) "Poets"

ALL-FINANCE TEAM

Captain Gene BANKS, Bulls
A. C. GREEN, Lakers
"BUCK" Johnson, Rockets
Brad SELLERS, Bulls
"BUCK" Williams, Nets
6th man - Mark PRICE, Cavs

Wes Unseld of the University of Louisville and the Baltimore Bullets.

What is the most formidable All-America team in history?

We choose the 1968 squad: Elvin Hayes, Houston; Wes Unseld, Louisville; Lucius Allen, UCLA; Don May, Dayton; Lew Alcindor, UCLA; Bob Lanier, St. Bonaventure; Pete Maravich, LSU; Larry Miller, North Carolina; Calvin Murphy, Niagara; and Jo Jo White, Kansas. All of these players went on to play in either the NBA or the ABA, and eight indisputably became stars.

ALL-RESTAURANT TEAM

Captain Darwin COOK, Bullets
Walter BERRY, Spurs
Dell CURRY, Jazz
Mark EATON, Jazz
Clark KELLOGG, Pacers

AMAZING FINAL TRIVIA QUESTION

Who was known as the "Owl Without a Vowel?"
(A) John Grythzysk, Marist
(B) Al Auhl, Owlton State
(C) Bill Mlkvy, Temple
(D) "Big Joe" Rhythm, Oswego State

ALL-THEOLOGICAL TEAM

Captain James WORTHY, Lakers
Jeff CROSS, Clippers
Robert PARISH, Celtics
David POPE, Supersonics
Ricky SOBERS, Supersonics

OWL QUIZ ANSWER

C. Bill Mlkvy, for obvious reasons, since his Temple team was nicknamed the Owls. He still stands 4th on the major-college list of single-game scoring highs with 73. Do you think he attended Temple just so he could have such an amazing nickname?

THE AMAZING ANIMAL NICKNAME QUIZ ANSWERS

1. H	7. A
2. K	8. D
3. E	9. F
4. C	10. I
5. J	11. G
6. L	12. B

THE AMAZING NICKNAME QUIZ ANSWERS — PART 2

11. Z	19. O
12. Q	20. R
13. T	21. Y
14. S	22. N
15. P	23. V
16. X	24. L
17. W	25. K
18. U	26. M

THE AMAZING NICKNAME QUIZ ANSWERS — PART 1

1. I	6. D
2. C	7. F
3. H	8. A
4. G	9. E
5. B	10. J

When that One Great Scorer finally came to write against James Naismith's name He surely must have known that The Doc had invented basketball. But even He must have been surprised at how far Naismith had left that tiny Springfield gymnasium behind him in pursuit of a full, rich and happy life.

It was a life that included Naismith's becoming a father of five, a doctor of medicine, and an ordained minister. The Doc also volunteered to serve his country during the Mexican War, and went to France during WWI to become a lecturer on, of all things, sex education.

The Doc did all that. He remained kind, gentle, generous, decent and unassuming to the end. His fame spread around the world, but he cared so little about making money that he twice lost houses to mortgage companies; a man with his credentials these days would be out making Lite Beer commercials.

The Doc wasn't always happy with what was happening to his game. To his death he never understood why so simple a sport should require much coaching, but he remained very proud that he had invented it.

Let's go back and pick up The Doc's trail just about where we'd lost it, on June 20, 1894, the day Naismith married Maude Evelyn Sherman in the Hope Congregational Church in Springfield.

Maude, you will remember, had played in the first women's basketball game at Springfield College. But The Doc had found an even better track to her hand than that; he'd lived at the Springfield boarding house operated by her parents.

The Naismiths were happy in Springfield. A baby girl, Margaret Mason Naismith, was born to them on July 1, 1895. However, The Doc was getting restless. He wanted to do more than invent basketball, which hadn't seemed like such a big deal at the time. He had decided after seeing so many sports injuries that he wanted to become a doctor.

At age 33, the former high school dropout wanted more education.

In 1895 he and Maude left Springfield for Denver, where Naismith would be director of physical education at the local YMCA and attend Gross Medical School.

For three years Naismith juggled his time between the directorship of the good, but financially troubled YMCA, and classes at Gross, which in time became part of the University of Colorado School of Medicine.

The times became even tougher when Maude Naismith, ill with typhoid fever during her pregnancy with their second child, lost most of her hearing. She had to learn to read lips and became something of a recluse for the rest of her life.

Opposite page: Dr. James Naismith and friends.

Their second child, Helen Carolyn Naismith, was born December 21, 1897. Weak and frail, the baby added to all the other pressures on the family, but all survived.

On April 8, 1898, The Doc became a medical doctor, but he never did hang out his shingle. He didn't want a doctor's office any more than he had wanted his own church; he just wanted the knowledge and the experience.

A few months later the fates that had followed Naismith all his life made another move. The University of Kansas had need, of all things, for one man to fill the combined role of chapel director, athletic director and head of the newly-formed department of physical education.

There stood James Naismith with a degree in theology, a degree in medicine and years of experience in physical education. The timing was especially good for The Doc, too; one of his young students had been accidentally killed in a YMCA tumbling class and Naismith had grieved for months.

He had prayed for change in his life and the answer came from an old friend, Amos Alonzo Stagg, who had recommended Naismith for the Kansas job.

So in the fall of 1898 the Naismiths were off to Lawrence, Kansas. The Doc was 36, his wife 28, they had two young children and they wanted to settle down. The Doc's salary was to be $1,300 a year.

Naismith soon learned athletics were not very important at the University of Kansas. There was some interest in football, but basketball was about as popular as jai alai; the school, in fact, didn't even have a basketball team.

Naismith quickly organized eight teams among the faculty and students. It wasn't part of his contract, but he also began coaching a university team. Its first home game was played in 1899 in a skating rink against the Topeka YMCA, with Kansas winning 31-6.

Those early Kansas teams played in Snow Hall, a gymnasium with an 11-foot ceiling that didn't leave much room for error. The Doc solved that problem by having the gym floor lowered five feet into the basement. His players then used a ladder to get up and down from the field of play.

Naismith had learned it was possible to lower the floor after following Mr. Crocker, a school janitor, into a basement storeroom.

The Doc never went wrong following janitors.

Naismith coached the Kansas team until 1912, hanging up his whistle with an overall coaching record of 53 wins and 55 losses.

Kansas, of course, has gone on to great success in college basketball. James Naismith, in fact, is the only losing coach the school has ever had!

Even without basketball Naismith stayed busy. He led chapel services. He was, for a time, the school's track coach. He added lacrosse to its program. He expanded his classroom teaching, moving into personal hygiene, child development, adolescent development and sex education, well ahead of his peers. He even, and this was back in 1909, rigged up some equipment to test the effects of alcohol on the nervous system.

On the community level, Naismith became a 32nd degree Mason, a Sunday school teacher, dispensed medical advice freely, and led social discussion groups in the living room of friends.

At home, the Naismiths had two more children, John Edwin Naismith, born November 3, 1900, and Maude Annie Naismith, born October 29, 1904.

The bad news in the midst of all this was that The Doc, never one to worry about income and bills, lost his house because he didn't make the payments.

Left: A rare photo of basketball's inventor taking a shot. Right: The Doc, always a busy man, takes a break from a construction job.

He just shrugged his shoulders and moved the family to another house.

Maude was almost 44 years old when James Sherman Naismith, their fifth and final child, was born on May 7, 1913. Two years after that — and 25 years after he had left seminary school — The Doc finally became an ordained minister. He did it by volunteering, at age 54, while still a Canadian citizen, to join the Kansas National Guard as chaplain.

Unfortunately, President Woodrow Wilson called up the National Guard in 1916 in retaliation for Mexican outlaw Pancho Villa's attacks into the United States. Suddenly The Father of Basketball was off to the South Texas border where, between his lectures on the evils of sin and prostitution, he set up a makeshift basketball court.

Naismith only served a few months in Texas. But when he got home America was poised to plunge into World War I. So The Doc, at 55, volunteered to work with the National War Work Council and the YMCA to strengthen the moral character of the American serviceman.

He was, in short, to be a member of the WWI sex-lecture circuit.

In September, 1917, The Doc sailed to France. Working with the YMCA, often near the mud and blood of the front, he delivered sex lectures, set up recreational activities and promoted armed forces basketball tournaments.

After a 19-month tour of duty, Naismith went back home to Kansas in April, 1919, to resume his teaching career. In May, 1925, both he and his wife became naturalized American citizens.

By then The Doc's glow had dimmed quite a bit around campus. Although he was still quite healthy at 63, the university had divided his old job among several younger men.

In the depression of the 1930s, The Doc, then earning $3,000 a year, fell behind on his payments and lost a second house. Some financially better-off colleagues had offered to help make payments, but Naismith wouldn't accept the offers.

He just moved to a third, much smaller house he had built as rental property.

The Doc still had one Huge Honor coming. In 1935 Phog Allen, then the very successful Kansas basketball coach, began a national campaign to raise money to send Naismith to the 1936 Olympic games in Berlin. There basketball would be played for the first time as an official Olympic sport. The idea to send him was soon adopted by the National Association of Basketball Coaches.

"Naismith Nights" were held at basketball games across America, with a penny from each ticket to go to The Doc's Olympic fund. By the spring of 1936 the fund, collected from 43 states, had reached nearly $5,000.

In July, 1936 — Maude was too sick to join him — Naismith set sail for Germany. He was on hand to toss up the ball in the first-ever Olympic basketball game, a clash between mighty Estonia and France.

Dr. James Naismith and his sons, Jack and Jim, with lacrosse gear at the University of Kansas campus. The Doc was an admirable family man. Although he badly needed the money, he turned down a lucrative endorsement from a tobacco company, saying its products were harmful to his children and grandchildren.

He was there, ironically, when the United States defeated Canada, his home country, 19 to 8 to win the championship. That gold medal game was played outdoors in the rain on a muddy court built of dirt and sawdust.

Naismith said the 1936 Olympics was his finest moment, absolute proof that the game he'd invented in a time of near desperation in a tiny training school gymnasium had made it fully around the world.

Six months later, on March 4, 1937, Maude Naismith, his wife of almost 43 years, died of a heart attack. Two months later, Naismith, at 75, partially retired from Kansas as a professor-emeritus.

On June 10, 1939, at age 77, he remarried. His new bride was Florence Kincaid, 56, who had been a housemother at a Kansas fraternity.

They did not have much time together. On November 19 of that year The Doc suffered a cerebral hemorrhage. He recovered, remarkably, in three days.

However, five days later he was hit with a second stroke. He died in his home at 1:50 a.m. on November 28, 1939. He was 78 years old.

Across America, another basketball season was beginning.

My greatest wish is that
my pen could adequately
express the feelings of my
heart for the honor and
opportunity that your
magnificent gift has
given me—

With kindest personal
remembrances and best
wishes for your success
I am

Most sincerely yours

James Naismith

Dr. Naismith wrote this letter to W. C. Chandler, basketball coach at Marquette and chairman of the national committee for the Naismith Fund to send The Doc to the 1936 Olympics.

The End.

Appendix

Here are 105 Amazing Events in the long and glorious history of basketball:

December, 1891 — Dr. James Naismith invents basketball at the School for Christian Workers in Springfield, Mass.

January 15, 1892 — First printed basketball rules appear in *The Triangle,* the magazine at the school.

March, 1892 — The first public game was played between the school's students and teachers. The students won 5-1 as 200 people watched. Amos Alonzo Stagg scored the teachers' only goal (There was previously a YMCA public game in Feb.).

1892 — Basketball began to move around the world as the game was introduced in Mexico.

1892 — Lew Allen of Hartford, Conn., made cylindrical baskets of woven wire, the first attempt to eliminate the flimsy peach baskets.

1893 — The first backboards, six feet by 12 feet in size, were introduced. They were necessary to stop the fans in the balconies from interfering with the ball.

March 22, 1893 — Smith College became the first women's school to play basketball. Since the girls were in bloomers, no men were allowed to watch the game.

1894 — The Overman Wheel Co. of Chicopee Falls, Mass., invented the first basketball. Until then, soccer balls had been used.

1894-95 — The free-throw line was shortened from 20 to 15 feet.

1895 — The free-throw was first introduced as a penalty for fouls.

February 9, 1895 — Hamline College of St. Paul, Minn., defeated the Minnesota State School of Agriculture 9 to 3 in the first-ever game between two college teams. There were nine players on each side.

April 4, 1895 — California and Stanford played the first known women's intercollegiate game. The score is not known.

1895-96 — The field goal was changed from three points to two points. The free throw was changed from three points to one point.

1895-96 — The backboard was officially reduced in size to four feet by six feet.

January 16, 1896 — The University of Chicago beat the University of Iowa (actually a local YMCA team) 15 to 12 in the first college game played with five on a side. Neither team substituted.

1896 — The first professional basketball game was played in Trenton, N.J.

1896-97 — Basketball rules were changed so a player could not dribble with two hands more than once.

1898 — The National Basketball League, the first professional basketball league, was formed. It included Trenton, N.J., Camden, N.J., Millville, Pa., the Pennsylvania Bicycle Club, the Hancock Athletic Club and the Germantown Club.

1901 — The rules stated that a dribbler could not shoot for a field goal; the ball had to be passed to another player.

1901 — Holyoke (Massachusetts) High School defeated the Mount Vernon (New York) High School at the Pan-American Exposition in Buffalo, N.Y., in the finals of the first national high school tournament.

1901-02 — The Triangular League, made up of Yale, Trinity and Wesleyan, became the first college conference.

1904 — Hiram College defeated Wheaton College 25 to 20 in the finals of a national college tournament held in conjunction with the Olympic Games in St. Louis.

1905 — Lawrence College in Wisconsin hosted the first state high school tournament. Fond du Lac was the winner.

1906 — New York's Madison Square Garden held its first basketball tournament.

1908 — A player committing five fouls (including travelling and other violations) was disqualified from the game.

1909-10 — Glass backboards were approved for the first time.

1909-10 — The rules were changed again so a player was disqualified from the game after his fourth foul.

1913-14 — The rules finally stated that the bottom of the basket must be left open so the ball could fall through.

1919 — The first international tournament was held in Paris. The United States eased past France in the finals, 93-8. James Naismith witnessed the game and Gen. John "Black Jack" Pershing presented the winning trophy to Hall of Fame player Max "Marty" Friedman.

1920 — The rules committee said a player could only re-enter a game once.

1920-21 — The backboards were moved two feet from the walls, stopping the practice of players' jumping up the walls to shoot.

1921-22 — "Traveling" with the ball, which had been considered a personal foul, was changed to a violation.

1923-24 — The rules were changed to say the player fouled had to shoot the foul shot. Prior to that each team had a designated free-throw shooter.

1926 — The Pasadena Athletic and Country Club hosted the first women's AAU tournament. It was played under men's rules, and the local Pasadena team won.

1927 — The Harlem Globetrotters played their first game in Hinckley, Illinois.

1929 — The practice of using a wire or rope cage around a court to keep the ball in play was ended.

1929-30 — The concept of having two referees in a game instead of one was officially adopted.

1932 — The ten-second line was created at mid-court to stop stalling, and no player *with the ball* was allowed to stand in the free throw lane more than three seconds.

June 18, 1932 — The International Amateur Basketball Federation was founded in Geneva, Switzerland.

1934-35 — The circumference of the ball, which once had been 32 inches, was reduced to between 29½ and 30¼ inches.

1936 — Basketball became an Olympic sport as the United States defeated Canada 19 to 8 in the finals in Berlin. The game was played outdoors in the rain.

December 30, 1936 — Stanford's Hank Luisetti popularized the one-handed shot in leading his team to a victory over Long Island University in Madison Square Garden. Before Luisetti, almost all shots were two-handed.

1936-37 — The rules were changed to prohibit any member of the offensive team, with or without the ball, from staying in the lane more than three seconds. The number of team timeouts was increased from three to four.

1937 — In this, the greatest year of all for rule changes, the center jump after each basket was eliminated, the defensive player was prohibited from touching the basket while the ball was on the rim, and the laceless ball was made legal.

March 12, 1938 — Warrensburg (Central Missouri State) won the first National Association of Intercollegiate Athletics (NAIA) tournament in Kansas City, beating Washburn College 45-30. The tournament is the oldest and biggest in the country.

March 17, 1938 — Temple defeated Colorado 60 to 36 in Madison Square Garden to win the first National Invitational Tournament.

March 28, 1939 — The University of Oregon beat Ohio State 46-33 in Evanston, Illinois, to win the first NCAA tournament.

November 28, 1939 — James Naismith died in Lawrence, Kansas, where he had coached and taught for about 40 years.

1939-40 — The backboards were moved four feet away from the end line — they had been two feet — to permit more movement under the basket.

February 28, 1940 — The first basketball games were televised from Madison Square Garden.

1940-41 — Fan-shaped backboards were made legal.

1944-45 The number of timeouts was increased from four to five. Unlimited substitution was permitted for the first time. The number of personal fouls leading to disqualification was increased from four to five. The goal-tending rule was expanded to prevent a defensive player from touching a ball on its downward flight.

1945-46 — Wyoming's Kenny Sailors is credited with inventing the jump shot, although others may have experimented with it.

June 6, 1946 — The Basketball Association of America, the forerunner of today's National Basketball Association, was formed.

1947 — The Philadelphia Warriors beat the Chicago Stags to win the first BAA title. The Warriors were led by Kentuckian Joe Fulks.

1948-49 — Rectangular glass backboards became official in college play.

1948-49 — Coaches were finally allowed to speak to the players during a timeout.

August 11, 1949 — The Basketball Association of America and the National League, another pro circuit, merged to form the NBA.

1949-50 — The molded basketball became the official ball.

1950 — Chuck Cooper of Duquesne was drafted by the Boston Celtics to become the first black drafted by the NBA.

November 22, 1950 — The NBA Fort Wayne Pistons defeated the Minneapolis Lakers 19-18 in the lowest-scoring game in NBA history.

1951 — A crowd of 75,000, the biggest in basketball history, watched the Harlem Globetrotters play a game in Berlin.

1952 — The foul lane was widened from six to 12 feet.

February 13, 1954 — Furman's Frank Selvy scored an even 100 points against Newberry in his team's 149 to 95 win to become the first major-college player to hit the century mark.

October 30, 1954 — The 24-second clock was used for the first time in an NBA game as Rochester defeated Boston 98-95.

1957-58 — The rules were changed to allow a team to shoot a bonus free throw once the opponents commit seven fouls in a half.

1957-58 — Oscar Robertson became the first sophomore to win an NCAA scoring title, averaging 35.1 a game for Cincinnati.

January 26, 1960 — Danny Heater of Burnsville, West Virginia, scored a national-record 135 points in a high school game as his team defeated Widen High School 173-43.

1960 — The Minneapolis Lakers moved to Los Angeles, giving professional basketball coast-to-coast coverage for the first time.

March 2, 1962 — Wilt Chamberlain scored 100 points in a professional game as his Philadelphia Warriors beat the New York Knicks 169-147.

1963-64 — Players assessed personal fouls were asked to raise their arms.

January 29, 1964 — Boone Trail High School of Mamers, North Carolina, defeated Angier High School 56-54 in 13 overtimes, then the scholastic record.

1966-67 — Bill Russell became the first black coach in the NBA.

1967 — The American Basketball Association, a rival to the NBA, began its first season.

1967-68 — Primarily because of Kareem Abdul-Jabbar, the dunk shot was banned from college basketball.

February 17, 1968 — The Naismith Memorial Basketball Hall of Fame opened in Springfield, Massachusetts, on the campus of Springfield College where the game had been invented.

1968 — The Pittsburgh Pipers beat the New Orleans Buccaneers four games to three to win the first ABA championship.

1971 — The number of players on women's basketball teams was reduced from six to five.

January 9, 1972 — The Milwaukee Bucks beat Los Angeles 120-104 to end the Lakers' 33-game win streak, an NBA record.

March 20, 1972 — Immaculata defeated West Chester State 52 to 48 to win the first Association for Intercollegiate Athletics for Women (AIAW) championship, considered the first true national women's championship.

1972 — Freshmen were allowed to play major-college basketball for the first time.

September 9, 1972 — The United States lost its first Olympic basketball game, falling to the USSR 51 to 50.

January 19, 1974 — Notre Dame ended UCLA's 88-game winning streak with a 71 to 70 victory at home.

August, 1974 — Moses Malone signed with the Utah Stars of the NBA to become the first modern pro player to go from high school to a professional league.

1976 — The dunk shot was returned to college basketball.

1976 — Women's basketball became an Olympic event for the first time. USSR team beat the Americans in the finals, 112 to 77.

1976-77 — The ABA folded and four of its teams, Denver, Indiana, New Jersey and San Antonio, went into the NBA.

December 9, 1978 — The short-lived Women's Professional Basketball League began with the Chicago Hustle beating the Milwaukee Does 92 to 87.

1978-79 — The NBA added a third referee.

1979-80 — The NBA added the three-point shot and dropped the third referee.

October 12, 1979 — Chris Ford of the Boston Celtics scored the NBA's first three-point field goal in his team's win over Houston.

November 29, 1980 — Ronnie Carr of Western Carolina scored the first collegiate three-point basket at 7:06 p.m. in a game against Middle Tennessee. Carr's Southern Conference team was using the three-point shot on an experimental basis.

January 23, 1981 — Annette Kennedy of SUNY-Purchase scored 70 points in a game against Pratt, setting the women's record.

1981-82 — College basketball restricts jump balls to the beginning of the game and the start of overtime periods. Teams alternate taking the ball out of bounds on other jump-ball situations.

December 21, 1981 — Cincinnati defeats Bradley 75 to 73 in seven overtimes at Peoria, Illinois, the Division I record.

March, 1982 — Louisiana Tech beats Cheyney State 76 to 62 to win first NCAA Division basketball championship for women.

July, 1984 — The United States' men's and women's teams win Olympic titles in the Los Angeles games.

1984-85 — The NCAA officially approves a smaller basketball for women's basketball. It is 29 inches in circumference, about an inch smaller than the men's ball.

December 21, 1984 — Georgeann Wells of West Virginia becomes the first woman to dunk a basketball in collegiate competition.

June 30, 1985 — The new $11.4 million Naismith Memorial Basketball Hall of Fame opens in downtown Springfield, Massachusetts.

1985-86 — The NCAA approves a 45-second shot clock for all men's games.

1986-87 — The United States' Pan-American team loses the championship game to Brazil.

1987-88 — The three-point shot is extended to women's and high school basketball.

Bibliography

Abel, Bob and Valenti, Michael. *Sports Quotes.* New York: Facts on File, Inc., 1983
All-Sports Record Book, 1932.
Barzman, Sol. *505 Basketball Questions Your Friends Can't Answer.* New York: Walker and Co., 1981.
Beirne, Gerald. *The New England Sports Trivia Book.* Dublin, N.H.: Yankee Publishing, 1983.
Bender, Jack H. *Basketball-Log.* St. Louis: Valley Publishing Co., 1959.
Berensen, Miss Senda. *Basketball For Women.* New York: American Sports Publishing Co., 1901.
Braine, Tim and Stravinsky, John. *The Not-So-Great Moments in Sports.* New York: Quill, 1986.
Brown, Gene. *The Complete Book of Basketball — A New York Times Scrapbook History.* New York: Arno Press, 1980.
Bruce, Robert M. *Annotated Bibliography of Basketball Literature.* National Association of Basketball Coaches, 1947.
Burnes, Robert L. *50 Golden Years of Sports.* St. Louis: Rawlings Manufacturing Co., 1948.
Caudle, Edwin C. *Collegiate Basketball.* Winston-Salem, N.C.: John F. Blair, 1960.
Clark, Patrick. *Sports Firsts.* New York: Facts on File, Inc., 1981.
Colbeck, Leslie. *The Basketball World.* International Amateur Basketball Federation, 1972.
Cole, Lewis. *A Loose Game.* Indianapolis: Bobbs-Merrill, 1978.
Frankhauser, Henry. *The Wacky World of Sports.* Cranbury, N.J.: A. S. Barnes and Co., 1968.
Fischler, Stan. *Marv Albert's Sports Quiz Book.* New York: Grosset & Dunlap, 1976.
Fox, Larry. *Illustrated History of Basketball.* New York: Grosset and Dunlap, 1974.
Gipe, George. *Great American Sports Book.* Garden City, N.Y.: Doubleday, 1978.
Green, Lee. *Sportswit.* Fawcett Crest, N.Y.: Ballantine, 1984.
Gulick. Luther. *The Official Basketball Guide.* New York: American Sports Publishing Co., 1899.
Henderson, Edwin Bancroft. *The Negro in Sports.* Associated Publishers, Inc., 1939.
Hirschberg, Al. *Basketball's Greatest Teams.* New York: Putnam, 1965.
Hollander, Phyllis. *100 Greatest Women in Sports.* New York: Grosset & Dunlap, 1976.
Hollander, Zander. *Modern Encyclopedia of Basketball.* New York: Four Winds Press, 1969.
Hollander, Zander. *Pro Basketball Encyclopedia.* Millerton, N.Y.: 1977.
Hoose, Phillip M. *Hoosiers.* New York: Vantage Books, 1986.
Isaacs, Neil D. *All the Moves.* Philadelphia: J. B. Lippincott Co., 1975.
Kindred, Dave. *Basketball, the Dream Game in Kentucky.* Louisville: Data Courier, Inc., 1976.
Koppet, Leonard. *24 Seconds to Shoot: An Informal History of the NBA.* New York: Macmillan Company, 1968.
Liss, Howard. *Strange but True Basketball Stories.* New York: Random House, 1972.
MacLean, Norman and Ecksl, Norb. *The Basketball Quizbook.* New York: Drake Publishers, 1976.

McCallum, John D. *College Basketball USA Since 1892.* Briarcliff Manor, N.Y.: Stein and Day, 1978.

McWhirter, Norris. *Guinness Book of Sports Records.* New York: Sterling, 1982.

Mendell, Ronald. L. *Who's Who in Basketball.* New Rochelle, N.Y.: Arlington House, 1973.

Naismith, James. *Basketball.* New York: Association Press, 1941.

National High School Sports Record Book. Kansas City, Mo. 1986.

The National Sports Review. Seattle: Preview Publishing, 1986.

1987 NCAA Basketball. Mission, Kansas: NCAA, 1987.

Neil, Randy and Hart, Elaine. *Official Cheerleaders' Handbook.* New York: Simon & Schuster, Inc.

Nemec, David. *Great Baseball Feats, Facts and Firsts.* New York: New American Library, 1987.

The Official Naismith Memorial Basketball Hall of Fame Souvenir Book. Springfield, Mass.: Hall of Fame/Bordeaux Co., 1987.

Pepe, Phil and Hollander, Zander. *The Book of Sports Lists #1, #2 and #3.* New York and Los Angeles: Pinnacle Books, 1980 and 1981.

Pratt, John Lowell and Benagh, Jim. *The Official Encyclopedia of Sports.* New York: Franklin Watts, Inc., 1964.

Reach Official Book of Basket Ball Rules. Philadelphia: A. J. Reach, Co., 1903.

Webb, Bernice Larson. *The Basketball Man: James Naismith.* The University Press of Kansas, 1973.

Whittingham, Richard. *The Final Four.* Chicago: Contemporary Books, Inc., 1983.

Yee, Min S. and Wright, Donald. *The Sports Book.* New York: Bantam Books, 1975.

Randall Baron, a long-time Louisville book publisher, has been a basketball fan since he was old enough to grow a mustache. He has co-authored books on bridge, horse racing *(The Official Kentucky Derby Quiz Book)* and basketball *(The Official University of Kentucky Basketball Book)*, and has never met an NCAA tournament or golf course he didn't like. He lives in his native Louisville with his wife, Mary, their two children, Devyn and Dustin, and their intelligent cocker spaniel, Victor. **Bob Hill,** a *Louisville Courier-Journal* columnist, was the tallest kid in his class 12 years in a row in Sycamore, Illinois, where he was named all-city his senior year. Hill, winner of a dozen regional and national journalism writing awards, including *"Best in Louisville,"* went on to a very undistinguished basketball career at Rice University. He lives in Utica, Indiana, with his wife, Janet, their two children, Jennifer and Robb, and a weedy garden.

ORDER FORM

Call

502-895-1354

in Kentucky

Call Toll Free (outside Kentucky)

1-800-626-1598

9 AM to 5 PM EST

VISA or MASTERCARD
ACCEPTED
or Mail to:
DEVYN PRESS, INC.,
151 Thierman Lane,
Louisville, KY 40207

☐ Devyn Press, Inc., is America's largest publisher of literature on the game of bridge. We will be happy to send a copy of our FREE catalog to you (and your friends) upon request. Simply check this box or ask for one (or more) when you call us.

Please send me _____ copies of "The Amazing Basketball Book", _____ copies of "The Official University of Kentucky Basketball Book" and _____ copies of "The Official Kentucky Derby Quiz Book." For each copy I enclose the correct amount (less appropriate discount) + a total of $2 for shipping/handling/ insurance for the order.

The Amazing Basketball Book $7.95 x _____ = $_____

Kentucky Derby Book $11.95 x _____ = $_____

UK Basketball $9.95 x _____ = $_____

QUANTITY DISCOUNT:
10% over $25
20% over $50
Less discount $_____

Subtotal $_____

We accept checks, money orders and charge card orders, send your card number and expiration date.
Shipping/Handling/ Insurance $2.00

Amount enclosed $_____

Name _____

Address _____

City _____ State _____ Zip_____

(WHOLESALE INQUIRIES ARE WELCOME)